Preaching in the Orthodox Church

Other books published by the Orthodox Research Institute include:

Saint Cyril of Alexandria. *Against Those Who Are Unwilling to Confess that the Holy Virgin Is Theotokos.* Introduction, Greek Text and English Translation by Protopresbyter George Dion. Dragas

Metropolitan Bishoy of Damiette. *The Real Holy Grail: An Orthodox Response to Dan Brown's Deceptions in Angels and Demons and The Da Vinci Code*

Rev. Dr. Steven Bigham. *Early Christian Attitudes toward Images*

Panagiotes K. Chrestou. *Greek Orthodox Patrology: An Introduction to the Study of the Church Fathers.* Edited and translated by Protopresbyter George Dion. Dragas

Protopresbyter George Dion. Dragas. *Ecclesiasticus I: Introducing Eastern Orthodoxy*

Protopresbyter George Dion. Dragas. *Ecclesiasticus II: Orthodox Icons, Saints, Feasts and Prayer*

Protopresbyter George Dion. Dragas. *The Lord's Prayer according to Saint Makarios of Corinth*

Protopresbyter George Dion. Dragas. *On the Priesthood and the Holy Eucharist: According to St. Symeon of Thessalonica, Patriarch Kallinikos of Constantinople and St. Mark Eugenikos of Ephesus*

Protopresbyter George Dion. Dragas. *Saint Athanasius of Alexandria: Original Research and New Perspectives*

Protopresbyter George Dion. Dragas. *St. Cyril of Alexandria's Teaching on the Priesthood*

Alphonse and Rachel Goettmann. *The Spiritual Wisdom and Practices of Early Christianity*

Protopresbyter John S. Romanides. *An Outline of Orthodox Patristic Dogmatics*, in Greek and English. Edited and translated by Protopresbyter George Dion. Dragas

Preaching in the Orthodox Church

Lectures and Sermons by a Priest of the Holy Orthodox Church

Sebastian Dabovich

Rollinsford, New Hampshire

Published by Orthodox Research Institute
20 Silver Lane
Rollinsford, NH 03869
www.orthodoxresearchinstitute.org

Originally published as: *Preaching in the Russian Church*, San Francisco, CA: Cubery and Company, Publishers, 1899.

ISBN 978-1-933275-22-2

*To the Parish Priests
and to
Their Assistants, the School Teachers of the
Church in America,
This Volume Is Respectfully Dedicated
by their brother, one who knows their labor
in the tilling of the soil and the
sowing of the seed.*

Speaking the truth in love. (Ephesians 4:15)

Publisher's Foreword

When I came across a copy of this book, which was first published in San Francisco in 1899, I had not yet heard of Fr. Sebastian Dabovich. After reading this book, however, it became apparent that Fr. Sebastian was not simply an Orthodox priest serving the immigrant communities that brought the Orthodox Faith to the shores of America. His words are timeless and are just as important today to Orthodox Christians as well as to those, especially in America, who are unfamiliar with the Orthodox Church.

The V. Rev. Archimandrite Sebastian Dabovich was born in San Francisco, California, in 1863 to Serbian immigrants, who gave him the name of Jovan. After he graduated from high school, he traveled to Russia, where he studied in the Saint Petersburg and Kiev Theological Academies. While in Russia in 1888, he was tonsured a monk, with the name of Sebastian, and ordained a hierodeacon. Fr. Sebastian returned to San Francisco and served as a hierodeacon until his ordination to the priesthood in 1892. As a priest, Fr. Sebastian became a true apostle to America, traveling across the country helping communities establish parish churches. In addition, he traveled across the globe, being guided by his love for the Church and hoping to enlighten the non-Orthodox with the true light of the Orthodox Church. Fr. Sebastian also wrote many sermons, lectures and books. Fr. Sebastian died while in Serbia in 1940. He was buried at the Zica Monastery by St. Nikolai Velimirovic. In September 2007, Fr. Sebastian's remains were transferred from the Zica Monastery to

St. Sava Serbian Orthodox Church in Jackson, California, which is one of the parishes that he founded. His tombstone reads: "The First Serbian American Orthodox Apostle."[1]

To repeat the words of His Grace Bishop Irinej (Dobrijevic) of Australia and New Zealand: "Holy Apostle Sebastian, pray for us!"

D.R.L.

---

[1] For more detailed accounts of Fr. Sebastian's life, see the following: Hieromonk Damascene, "Archimandrite Sebastian Dabovich: Serbian Orthodox Apostle to America," *The Orthodox Word*; Mirko Dobrijevic (now Bishop Irinej of Australia and New Zealand, "The First American Serbian Apostle — Archimandrite Sebastian Dabovich," *Again*, vol. 16, no. 4 (December 1993); various articles in *The Path of Orthodoxy*, vol. 42, no. 10 (October 2007).

Preface

In this book, I offer to the English-speaking public in general, and to the American in particular, a historic, theological, and moral review of the Orthodox Eastern Apostolic Church, commonly called the Greek-Russian Church, in the form of lectures and sermons, thus enabling them to see the actual practice and teaching of a Church which is making herself at home in the West, notwithstanding her birth in the East, and which knows none other head but Jesus Christ.

Now and then people are told, chiefly through small journalism, that the Emperor of Russia is the head of the Orthodox Church. There are some who accept this view, and these belong to two classes: the uninformed and the prejudiced. It must be made clear that the Orthodox Church has three of her Patriarchs residing in the Turkish Empire, while about 6,000,000 of her members are the subjects of the Emperor of Austria, besides which we have to count the Kingdom of Greece, the Church in Egypt, and three independent branches of the Church in the Balkan States. We simply mention the purely characteristic Orthodox Church in Japan, the missions in China, America, and elsewhere, together with the Church's congregations in all the countries of Europe, which, though peculiarly original, in regard to their local premises, are, nevertheless, in spiritual relationship with the Great Church of Holy Russia, relying upon her for the larger portion of their support. And the Russian Church, enjoying in complete measure the sympathy of the Orthodox and highly pious Ruler of the Empire, does not begrudge Orthodox missions her support, which is so often made the subject for taunting with suspicions by outsiders who are strangers to the Christian spirit of toleration. Thus, it is clear that the Orthodox Church has no Pope-head; she is not a monarchy, but as the Church of Christ, she is Catholic and Apostolic. Indeed, it would seem strange to say that in this country Queen Victoria is the head of the Episcopal Church, because the Anglican and Episcopal Churches are in close communion.

Readily do we acknowledge, and sometimes too hastily adopt, the results of the great achievements of the Western mind and spirit in the affairs of this world; but in matters of faith the Eastern is, as it has ever been, the source and cradle of everything that is purest, highest, and heavenly. Humiliating though it might appear to the haughty spirit of the West, it will at last, and of necessity, turn its eyes towards the East and realize the saying: *Ex Oriente lux*!

SEBASTIAN DABOVICH
A priest of the Holy Orthodox Church,
San Francisco, on the day of our Lady of Kazan, 1899

Table of Contents

PUBLISHER'S FOREWORD i

PREFACE iii

THE IMMORTALITY OF THE SOUL 1

THE NECESSITY FOR DIVINE REVELATION AND
THE INDICATIONS OF A REVEALED RELIGION 9

THE AUTHENTICITY AND TRUTHFULNESS OF THE GOSPEL 17

THE TRUE CHURCH OF CHRIST 33

THE EDUCATION OF CHILDREN 41

SERMON ON NEW YEAR'S DAY 45

THOUGHTS ON FAST AND TEMPERANCE 51

SERMON ON THE GOSPEL OF THE PRODIGAL 57

SERMON PREACHED ON ORTHODOX SUNDAY 61

SERMON PREACHED ON THE THIRD SUNDAY
OF GREAT LENT 65

SERMON FOR THE FOURTH SUNDAY IN GREAT LENT 69

THOUGHTS FOR GOOD FRIDAY AT THE PASSIONS
AND BURIAL OF CHRIST 73

SERMON ON THE GOSPEL RELATING TO THE IMPOTENT 77

SERMON FOR THE SUNDAY WHEN THE GOSPEL
OF THE BLIND IS READ 83

SERMON ON THE FEAST OF THE ASCENSION 87

SERMON PREACHED ON TRINITY SUNDAY 91

THE CONDITION OF SOCIETY 95

SERMON TO THOSE PREPARING FOR HOLY COMMUNION 99

ADDRESS ON CHRISTMAS DAY 103

The Immortality of the Soul

God is not the God of the dead, but of the living: for all live unto Him (Luke 20:38)

There are many proofs testifying to the immortality of the soul, and they differ by degrees of strength, and the source from whence they proceed. There are proofs of supposition, then positive ones, and, finally, decisive proofs. We have some in visible nature, others are had from the attributes of God's being, and from the nature of our soul, and then there are open and experimental proofs.

What do we see in nature? A change of one and the same being from one condition to another higher form of existence. This is observed more clearly, especially, in the world of insects. Take, for an instance, the creeping worm and the flying butterfly, etc. In the same manner does man here on earth undergo two principal forms of life, to say nothing of his ages.

First, he is formed and lives unconsciously in his mother's womb, then, on being born into the world, he lives on the earth. This life is incomparatively higher than the first, yet here the days for man are exchanged by dark nights; after days of good fortune, there come days of misfortune. It is natural for him to await a third and better life, when he will freely move in the space over the earth, where it is eternal day, and where there is no sorrow nor sighing.

Of course, this proof is suppositional, but it contains no small degree of convincing power. The Lord Himself has implanted in our nature types and foretellings of the better life which is to come.

We also see that the animal kingdom, and man as well, are gifted with a generic immortality. By transmitting life from generation to generation, they will last as long as the earth continues in its present condition. And why cannot God give to the highest of all creatures, and to him who rules over all animals — i.e., to man — besides a generical also a personal immortality? The Lord is all-powerful. He can create everlasting beings. He is all-good, and the best good is a life which has no end and knows no grief.

The highest being on earth — i.e., man — were he not destined everlastingly to glorify the eternal God, and were he not immortal, the earth would be a sorrowful spectacle of the all-destroying and all-devouring death, and God would be only the God of the dead, and not of the living upon earth.

There are yet other proofs of the immortality of the soul, which rest upon two principles combined: First, the existence and attributes of God; second, upon the nature of the soul.

The first positive and clear proof of this kind is the following: Without a doubt, there is a God, because He reveals Himself to man, not only in his soul, but in visible nature, and by a direct manifestation of Himself. He is a being all-just, all-holy. In the nature of man's soul, He has implanted the aspiration for good deeds and the aversion for evil; and there are many people who try to do right and accomplish holy deeds, while at the same time, they bear heavy trials of self-renouncement. Yet we see on earth that sinners often enjoy good fortune and success, and the just suffer until death, and mostly at the hands of sinners.

If there were no other life for people, in which there must be a reward according to actions, then God would not be all-just and holy. He would not be merciful to the good, while showing mercy to the unjust ones, and this cannot be conceived of God. Therefore, as God is holy, there will be another life, in which the sinners and the righteous will receive their just reward.

Another proof of the immortality of the soul is like this, but wider in its contents. In the mind of man, God has implanted a desire for the truth, in his will a striving for the good, in his heart an inspiration for happiness; but the mind of man does not become satisfied with the knowledge obtained on earth. He sees that it is not, by far, complete and perfect. His will meets with much resistance in growing in the good. Although man labors much for the good while on earth, yet he finds himself, by far, undeveloped in a moral sense; he feels the burden of sin; his heart finds no true blessedness on earth. The thought of eternity and the everlasting is rooted in our soul. It is not only that the soul possesses the idea of the infinite and most high Being, but with the heart and will itself, it yearns to approach Him.

Furthermore, what meaning is there in the fact that people, by different ways, endeavor to perpetuate their name upon the earth, desiring to be remembered as long as possible after their death?

All mankind, with the exception of a few individuals, believe in the future life. Why should the Creator implant in the spirit of man such lofty aspirations, if they were not to be realized, if such hopes were not fulfilled and desires not satisfied — i.e., if there were no better, everlasting existence? It would not be according to the goodness, and the wisdom, and the holiness of the Almighty, of which we know.

Therefore, as it is beyond doubt that there is an eternal and all-perfect God, it is also beyond doubt that there will be a life without end for man, in which the longings of his spirit, or soul, will be satisfied.

Also, many uncommon manifestations of the powers of the soul prove its non-materialistic and everlasting qualities. Such are: Predictions of events in the future; visions of what is going on in another part of the earth, at a great distance; and distinct foresight of the future, sometimes at a very long period in advance, and most often in images, not only in sleep, but also in a wakeful condition.

The most definite and decisive proofs of the immortality of the soul are the theological ones which we have from Divine Revelation, and also experimental ones, in the appearance of the souls of people who are dead.

God has many times revealed Himself to people, in different ways, and He still does so, through His saints, chiefly in prophecies, signs, and miracles. But why has He revealed Himself to people, and does so still? He has and yet does so in order to prepare us for the next blessed life.

God has not only revealed Himself to mankind, but He has shown us the way and the means by which to attain the better, heavenly life.

The Lord, in His revelation, says that the soul will live eternally, that it will never die, and that man, in his very body, after the resurrection of the dead, cannot die (Luke 20:36).

It would fill a large book to relate all the appearances of the soul known of in the ancient world. And since the time of Christianity, you have read or heard of the miracles in the lives of the saints.

If we were to gather authentic facts pertaining to visions from the spirit world in a period nearer to our day, why, they would make up several volumes. Not only saints have appeared, but sinners, and the souls of common people were revealed on earth for the knowledge and the assuring of the living in the existence of a future life.

Although it is forbidden Christians to thrust themselves, of their own accord, reaching out for still more evidence, into the spirit world, as well as it is strictly condemned by the Church systematically to practice the occult sciences, yet, on an occasion like this one, we may, for your proper information, relate, of the many, at least a few such instances.

When the Queen of Sweden, Ulrica, had died in the castle of Gripsholm, her body was laid in a coffin, and in the front room, a company of the Royal Guards were on duty. Punctually at noon-time there appeared in the parlor the Countess Steinbok, from the capital of Stockholm, whom the Queen had loved, and the commander of the Guards led her to the body of the Queen, and left her there.

As she did not soon return, the Captain opened the door, but, struck with horror, he fell back. On running to his aid, the officers then present saw, through the open door, the Queen, who was standing in her coffin, and embracing the Countess Steinbok. The vision seemed to float, and then changed into a heavy mist. When it soon cleared off, the body of the Queen was lying in the coffin, and the Countess Steinbok was nowhere to be found in the castle.

At once a messenger was dispatched with information of this incident to Stockholm, but word came back, that the Countess had not left the capital, and that she died at the time when they saw her in the embrace of the Queen.

Immediately a statement of the facts was written down, and signed by all who saw this vision.[1]

Much has been written of the appearances of the *white woman*, at different times, in the palaces and castles of Germany, foretelling the death of a member of the royal family. Judging from a portrait which was found, she proved to be the Princess Bertha von Rozenberg, who lived in the fifteenth century.

In December, 1628, she went through the apartments and halls of the Berlin mansion, and distinctly pronounced these words: "Come, Thou Judge of the living and the dead. There is yet hope of a judgment for me." During the present century, she appeared to the Queen Louise twice, and later on — on other occasions, which you may remember, having read of it in the newspapers.

Leaving these narratives, of which there are many in the histories of all nations, we shall now take up some facts, which are more appealing and pleasant, for the reason that they concern persons who are especially dear to us, being members of the Orthodox Church of Christ.

In 1855, there lived in the town of Epiphany, in the Russian province of Tula, a merchant, by name Basil Ivanov R., who held the office of church-warden at the cathedral. His family consisted of himself, his wife, two sons — Nicholas, 23 years of age, and married; John, 17 years old — and three daughters — Catherine, 13 years; Raisa, 11; and Alexandra, 6 years.

On the 10th of April, 1855, which was on the eve of the Sunday of the Holy Myrrh-bearing Women, Raisa, from fright, was suddenly taken with strong convulsions, while at the same time she evoked curses against God and His saints, but especially against St. Sergius. Medical aid afforded no relief to the unfortunate child.

Two months after the disease began, on the 11th and 12th of June, Raisa was taken with still more terrible convulsions. Becoming con-

---

[1] See the second edition of Dr. Shalberg's book, p. 63.

scious, she said that St. Sergius appeared to her, that he talked with her, and brought her a church loaf, which she ate. It seemed as though she ate, her relations said, but they could not see the *prosphora*, and attributed this to her sickness. The unbelief of her oldest brother, Nicholas, was especially painful to the girl.

In response to the instructions of St. Sergius, she requested all in the house to repeat the prayer, *May God arise*, and to make the sign of the cross. With great difficulty the mother set her fingers and made the sign of the cross upon her. It appeared to her that evil spirits were leaving her, as she saw, on making the form of the cross.

By another intimation from St. Sergius, an image of himself was found in the corner behind the sacred pictures, and this was put upon her.

Desiring to convince her brother of the fact of the appearance of the holy man with a church loaf, she asked for a glass of clean water, and taking some of the water into her mouth, she let it out again. Then could be seen crumbs of white bread in the water, which no one had given her.

After this she announced that the saint would come to her on the 13th date. At eleven o'clock in the evening of the appointed day, another spasm most frightfully shook her. In half an hour after, she arose and said, "Here comes St. Sergi," and then went to the window. Having opened the window, she let out her arms and began talking to someone. After this, she turned to her brother, and giving him something in a paper, tells him to hold it with reverence, as something holy. Then was given her, from below the window, a cross made of white ribbons. After showing it, she said that she was told to return it. At this, her face became bright. Her parents and the home folk at the same time felt a happiness and reverent fear.

Notwithstanding all their requests to give them the cross, she let it down in her hand out of the window, and it disappeared. The family ran out of the house, which was a one-story building, began to look for the cross under the window, but could not find it.

After this, she requested her brother to show what he held in his hand. There was found in the paper a corner-formed particle of a church loaf and some pieces of incense. Upon the paper, these words were written: "It is Thou, O Lord."

On being questioned by her relations, she said that St. Sergius came to her in company with a beautiful lad who was girdled with a deacon's stole. The holy man took out from under his cloak a napkin, out of which he gave her the paper and the cross. The paper with the prosphora and incense he ordered to be kept, but the cross to be returned. He also gave instructions that the girl's relations should believe, especially the brother Nicholas. Concerning the lad who appeared with him, he said: "He will guard you."

After this, the sick girl became entirely well. The next year, in June, 1856, she traveled with her mother and sister to the Troitsa Monastery, or Lavra of St. Sergi, near Moscow, and her mother told the superiors of all that happened. The particle of church bread, which she brought with her, proved to be the baking of the Monastery.

These events were written down, and as facts, they were attested to by the signatures of the girl's father, mother, and brother, and then by the archpriest, the priest, and the deacon of the St. Nicholas Cathedral in Epiphany, by each separately. Still this occurrence was not published in print for six years, only after six years, when it was learned that Raisa still continued in good health, it was published with the consent of Metropolitan Philaret in the journal of the Theological Academy of Moscow. This appearance of St. Sergius occurred 464 years after his death.

In 1812, when Napoleon entered Moscow, Prince Eugene, the Viceroy of Italy, with a division of warriors left Moscow for Zvenigorod to pursue the Russian partisans. The Prince occupied rooms in the Monastery of St. Sava, who was a pupil of St. Sergius of Radonezh. About ten o'clock, the Prince, without undressing, lay down and fell asleep. In the meantime, he sees a man in a long black habit — whether asleep now or awake, he did not know; by the light of the moon, he could see the man walk close up to him; he was old, with a grey beard. Then the visitor said to him: "Give thy men orders not to plunder the monastery; especially see that they take nothing from out the church.

If thou compliest with my wish, then God will have mercy upon thee, and thou shalt return to thy fatherland well and in safety."

Next morning the prince gave command that the division should return to Moscow; first, on going into the church, he saw by the tomb of St. Sabbas a picture of the man who appeared to him, and recognizing the image he reverently knelt before the relics of the saint and then took down in his diary a note of all that happened.

All the marshals of Napoleon came to their end unfortunately, but Eugene remained safe and was nowhere wounded in a battle after this. He expressed his will to his son Maximilian that, should he ever visit Russia, to go and offer his veneration at the tomb of St. Sabbas. The son came to Russia in 1839, during the reign of Emperor Nikolai Pavlovich, and after the military maneuvers on the field of Borodina, in memory of the battle of 1812, he inquired of the whereabouts of the Monastery of St. Sava, went there with guides, and knelt before the grave of the holy man. This event is so well known in history that there can be no doubt.

And so, this earth is a place for our temporal residence. It is the nursery of reasonable beings for other worlds. Thus, we will, and may be soon, taken from the earth. Let us pray the Lord, that He give us strength to leave our sins, which bring us down into the dark spaces of the universe, and that He help us to accomplish deeds which take us up into the high, eternally bright mansions of heaven. Amen.

The Necessity for Divine Revelation, and the Indications of a Revealed Religion

> *As you believe not Me, believe the works which I do, that ye may know and understand that the Father is in Me, and I in the Father, saith our Lord to the unbelieving Jews.* (John 10:38)

There are many religions in the world, and each people separately seem to be convinced that they hold the true faith, which was established by God. Why is it that the different races of mankind consider their faith to be the one Divinely revealed? It is because God has revealed Himself to the first people created by Him; then, during the course of time, He revealed Himself to the better people, informing them, and others through them, of His holy will. Fifteen centuries before the birth of Christ, during the time of Moses, God made known His holy will, through Balaam the prophet, who lived in the midst of pagans. About this time, or somewhat earlier, God appeared — for His presence individually may be revealed — to Job and his friends. But sooner than this, when nations began to leave God, and corrupted, by injurious notions, the revealed religion, — then it was that evil spirits commenced to deceive them with their revelations. Finally, there were persons, also, who, abusing the confidence and belief of others in Divine Revelation, falsely, but craftily, set up themselves as messengers from God.

Why did God, from the beginning, reveal Himself to people? Because, as we have said, the natural knowledge of the human mind concerning God, even before the fall of man, has not the strength, the precision, and the completeness; yet man is responsible for his actions: he is obliged to answer for his attitude toward God, to other people, and to himself. Therefore, all people in general believe only in a revealed religion. Some people foolishly say, God has given man a mind, and that is enough for him. But has not man, even besides his mind, many other teachers, in the persons of his parents, teachers, and guardians? Why should it be against reason to have as our teacher God Himself in those things which pertain to God?

Further, experience shows that mankind is in a disordered condition, out of which it cannot help itself. Is it natural that people, who are considered educated, while not believing in Divine Revelation, should, in matters of knowledge concerning the Divine, separate into parties which are opposed to one another?

1. A certain party, in defiance of sound reason, says that God, and His law given to people, do not exist; but they suppose that matter, with its invisible power (nevertheless, it is supposed by them that matter has its invisible power and law), has existed forever, and that the world and our living is not controlled by a reasonable Lawgiver.

2. There are some which say that everything in the world is God; all the things which we can see, they say, are the expression of the invisible soul of the world, which is unconscious, and gets to know itself by an evolution in the different forms of life. These so-called theosophists thereby ascribe to God Himself all the failures, defects, and crimes which proceed from people's abuse of liberty. Other faults of these false teachings have been pointed out before.

3. Yet there are others, who recognize God as an infinite, *perfect spirit*, the Creator of the universe; but they do not consider Him as the provider of the world, claiming that God, having created the world, gave it at the time, once for always, wise laws, and that He does not any longer concern Himself immediately about the world, but, say they, it governs itself by the laws given to it.

There have been, and there are such people still, who worship, not one, but many gods, and, at that, not only good ones, but also evil ones, which are opposed one to another. To what inconsistencies does not the fallen reason come, when left to itself in matters which pertain to the knowledge of God! And it thus continues for many thousand years, and it seems there will be no end to the disputes, in deciding the most important questions concerning God and the world, among the wise ones of this world; because to the natural powers and mind of man there is a fixed limit. Take, for instance, the natural sciences; i.e., the different studies about the visible world.

Let man perfect the instruments necessary for examining the things of this earth; let him discover new powers and laws which were not known to him before; let him enlarge the astronomical lens, and see new starry worlds — yet in all this he will see only matter with force in action, although according to wise laws, nevertheless according to laws of necessity; and one learned man, such as Newton, will pay homage at the very name of the Creator, while another, such as Leland, will sacrilegiously declare that he did not see God, even through the telescope. What do the sciences say of man? Should we not take the words of Moses concerning the beginning of the human race as Divinely revealed, then, for the want of other historical monuments, the beginning of mankind and the first ages would be covered under darkness of the perfectly unknown, and there would be no end to the conjectures and disputes concerning the beginning of people, the differences of race and languages, etc.

Further, can the science of the soul explain and decide these questions: How is the soul born of the souls of parents? How does the soul act upon the body? And how is it that the soul influences the body?

God Himself, to ends which are most wise, has ordered it so that the soul's action upon the body, and that of the body upon the soul, and the connection between them, should remain beyond the reach of our self-conscience. If man does not know how it is that the soul influences the body, then how may he expound and define the questions, How did the infinite, Divine Spirit bring forth this visible, material world? And how does He act upon it? Therefore, the sound reason of nation's calls for a faith, and demands a revealed religion; and

God actually revealed Himself to people, which for them was and is necessary, as they cannot attain to such knowledge by their own limited powers. Amazingly much is the feebleness of mind in defining the highest questions of knowledge. No less feeble is the fallen will in accomplishing good and unselfish works without special help from God. This has always been recognized by the best representatives of mankind. St. Paul the Apostle has written: *For the good which I would, I do not; but the evil which I would not, that I practice. For I delight in the law of God after the inward man; but I see a different law in my members, warring against the law of my mind, and bringing me into captivity under the law of sin* (Rom. 7:19, 22, 23). The philosopher Seneca, who lived in the same age, asks, "What does it mean? For when we desire one thing, we are drawn by a something to another." Another learned pagan, Ovid, of the same century, has written: "We always strive after that which is forbidden, desiring the prohibited. I see and value the better, but I follow the worse." Thus, as there is a God, it is beyond doubt, also, that His revelation and help to man, in regard to the knowledge of the Divine, and in striving to please God, is necessary, and we have strong reasons to show that, of all religions, the Christian belief is the only one true faith, established by God Himself for the salvation of people; and the Christian may say with the holy Apostle Paul, *I thank my God by Jesus Christ; the law of the spirit of life in Christ Jesus has liberated me from the law of sin and death* (Rom. 7:25; 8:2).

What are the proofs for the Divine character of the Christian religion? They are of two kinds. Some are contained in the investigation of the qualities of the Christian religion. The Christian doctrine is the purest and most elevated in comparison with the teachings of other beliefs. In other religions the ideas of God, and His attributes, and His relations to the world, are not consistent with sound reason, while Christians believe in the Lord God as the most supreme Spirit, with a nature which is most perfect, eternal, everywhere present, most wise, all-knowing, all-powerful, most good, all-holy, all-just, most blessed. Although there are mysteries in the Christian faith, such as are the two principal ones, namely, the trinity of persons in One, of the same

Godhead, and the incarnation of the Son of God, which are in most part incomprehensible to the mind; of course it is natural, as God in His substance is incomprehensible; yet they do not contain, in themselves, anything which is contrary to sound reason, but have sides that our mind understands. The Christian doctrine of the future life and the resurrection is also pure and elevated.

The moral law of the Christian religion is so perfect and exalted, that nothing more could be added to it. In regard to God, the law of Christ commands a filial love, which may prompt even the self-sacrifice of one's life for the glory of God, if needs be. Jesus Christ has given us a commandment, by which we are obliged to have a complete love toward our neighbor: *Love your enemies, bless those who curse you, and pray for those who do wrong to you and persecute you, that you may be the children of your heavenly Father* (Matt. 5:44, 45). *This is My commandment, that you love one another, as I have loved you* (John 15:2). And Christ died for people, when they were sinners — enemies of God. Finally, in regard to themselves, the law of Christ teaches that Christians must be humble, patient, self-sacrificing.

Still, the proof of the truth of religion because of its elevated teaching about God and the future life, and because of the purity of its moral law, is not yet the final decision, because even the most exalted teaching may be taken as the invention of man.

The most certain and definite proofs of the Divine character of a faith are the immediate testimonies of God Himself that the belief is true. The testimonies, therefore, must be revelations of a supernatural order, such as the manifestation of the Deity, prophecies, and genuine miracles. When God Himself appears to mankind, saying that this faith is the true one, or tests its truth by miracles, then, of course, we may not doubt it.

But, in other pagan religions, there have been, and yet may be, revelations, prophecies, and miracles worked by evil spirits; therefore the revelations of God, prophecies and miracles also, may not be, as it appears, sure proofs. In this instance, attention must be given to the power, and majesty, and character of the miracles.

Not being able to deny the miracles of Christ, the Pharisees — His enemies — said that He worked miracles, and even cast out devils, by the power of a higher evil spirit. But the Lord answered them, that the kingdom which is divided in itself cannot stand. He cast out thousands, or legions, of demons at once. Moreover, He worked such miracles which could not be performed by evil spirits.

When He gave sight to him that was born blind, the Jews, quarreling among themselves, said: *Can the Devil open the eyes of the blind?* (John 10:21). Some of the Pharisees themselves said: *A sinful man cannot work such miracles.*

Finally, the Lord resurrected the dead, and He Himself rose from the dead and ascended into heaven.

Secondly, where the evil spirits act, there the teaching concerning God is impure, for it is polytheism (like the pagans have) or pantheism, and the moral teaching is defective.

The evil spirits have succeeded in bringing people to deify sins and passions. The ancient nations had gods of wine, adultery, theft, and other hideous things. Therefore, two kinds of witnesses together are necessary; a faith is true, Divinely revealed, which, in the first place, is holy, pure, and exalted, and opposed to evil spirits, and which, secondly, is proved by revelations and miracles, and by miracles noted for their great power, and of which there are none in other religions; moreover, such ones which put the evil spirits to shame, being driven out of places in which they have ruled.

But, as miracles chiefly demonstrate the truthfulness of a faith, as they serve as witnesses for God Himself, and as unbelievers use all means to overthrow them, it is necessary, therefore, to set our attention upon them as proofs of the Divine character of the Christian religion.

In regards to Divine testimonies or miracles, no religion on earth may compare with Christianity. Miracles, witnessing to the heavenly origin of the Christian faith, come from the very beginning of the human race down to our time.

During 5,500 years — the time of the Old Testament — mankind has been preparing — being educated through supernatural revelations and miracles — to receive the Divine Organizer of our faith. Time will not permit to enumerate the miracles of ancient times. Just now we regret that we cannot give, as we should, special attention to the great number of Old Testament prophecies concerning Jesus Christ, as applying directly to His person. The miracles of our Lord Jesus Christ, which He worked Himself, have been explained to you on many occasions, and in the future, no doubt, they will continue to be a live source for exhaustless themes of instruction.

We hope to be granted the privilege to explain for you, in a short while, other proofs, demonstrating the truthfulness of the Gospels, and finally, with God's help, we will consider Orthodoxy as a sacred distinction in the midst of many Christian professions.

There are such people among Christians who are ashamed of miracles. Such Christians are ashamed of and deny Christ Himself; and He Himself will renounce them before His heavenly Father. Our Lord Jesus Christ, during His life on earth, has often pointed to miracles as to clear and definite proofs of His Divine mission.

While John the Baptist was confined in prison, he sent two of his disciples, for their as well as our benefit, to question Jesus: *Art Thou He that cometh, or look we for another? And Jesus answered them, Go and tell John the things which ye do hear and see: the blind receive their sight, and the lame walk, the lepers are cleansed, and the deaf hear, and the dead are raised up, and the poor have good tidings preached to them; and blessed is he, whosoever shall find none occasion for stumbling in me* (Matt. 11:2, 3, 4, 5, 6).

At another time, He said to the Jews, who believed not in Him, but among whom there were many who recognized John the Baptist as a saint: *I have witness which is greater than John's; the works which the Father hath given Me to fulfill, these same works which I do, bear witness of me, that I was sent by the Father* (John 5:36; 10:38).

St. John, the Forerunner of Christ, was not granted the power to work miracles, no doubt because the light of Christ must shine for a dark world the clearer of itself.

Many, says St. John the Apostle, *came to Jesus and said, that John hath done no miracle* (John 10:41).

Of His followers, our Lord said, in the last conversation with His disciples: *Believe me that I am in the Father, and the Father in Me: or else believe Me for the sake of the very works. Verily, verily, I say unto you, he that believeth on Me, the works that I do shall he do also; and greater works than these shall he do: because I go unto the Father* (John 14:11, 12).

And before His ascension into the heavens, He said to the Apostles: *These signs shall follow them that believe: in My name shall they cast out devils; they shall speak with new tongues; they shall take up serpents, and if they drink any deadly thing, it shall in no wise hurt them; they shall lay hands on the sick, and they shall recover* (Mark 16:17, 18).

O Lord! We are unworthy that Thy wonderful powers be made manifest upon us, as they have been and still do exhibit themselves through Thy saintly followers. Increase our faith in Thy works, which Thou hast performed for our salvation, and in the miracles of Thy saints. Set us aright, O Lord! and save us. Amen.

The Authenticity and Truthfulness of the Gospel

A s you are aware, we have the Gospel of our Lord Jesus Christ in the four books of the holy Evangelists: Matthew, Mark, Luke, and John. Whole libraries of books sprung up, as it were, from under the pens of the most eminent scholars of the world in defense of the authenticity of our accepted Gospel. Volume upon volume may, and in fact are, still being written, in proof of the truthfulness of the exposition we have of the work and teaching of our Lord Jesus Christ as laid down in the Gospel. Even the heathen with their dark histories and mysterious traditions have contributed to explain from more than one side *the hope of the nations, the glory of Israel, the light of the world.* If you are truly educated and take interest in this special line of study, you can freely make these investigations for yourself. Unfortunately, some who are affected with unbelief undertake the investigation of the Gospel, and the narratives about the miracles of Jesus Christ, with the express purpose, not of learning the truth, but in order to denounce them. These few persons (whose minds in every case were not intended by nature to be critical) are predetermined and have their minds previously biased with a false philosophy, so that, according to their fixed logic, there can be no miracles; therefore, they must be overturned by all possible means, and they have used everything within reach of their power against them, but they could gain no results.

Some of the unbelievers in miracles acknowledge that the Gospels were written by the Apostles themselves, or from the words of the

Apostles, as the Church believes, while others contend that the Gospels, although they bear up the names of the Apostles and their disciples, were not written by themselves, but by others, who lived later.

If the Apostles themselves have written the Gospels and described the miracles of Jesus Christ, then the unbelievers may yet have these two explanations for doing away with miracles. First — the Apostles have agreed among themselves to preach and to write falsehood. But it cannot be possible that the Apostles should alone agree to do such a thing, because many Christians who lived in their time would also have to acknowledge and preach the untruth. They could not attempt such a daring falsity, because they would be accused by the contemporaries of Jesus Christ; and why should they agree to such a thing, when — for their preaching Christ — nothing else but sorrow awaited them on earth? Besides this, God would punish them in the future life for the falsehood — especially in such an important matter. If we only in this life hope in Christ, then we are the most unfortunate of all people — thus writes St. Paul the Apostle to the Corinthians (1 Cor. 15:15, 19). Secondly — some other unbelievers contended that the Apostles did not understand the works of Jesus Christ, and that which was not miraculous, but natural, yet remarkable, in the life of Christ, they received as the miraculous. Nevertheless, the healing of the blind, the deaf, the lame and other incurables, even at an invisible distance, only by a word; the changing of the water into wine, the walking upon the sea, the feeding of five thousand people with five loaves, the raising of the dead, His own resurrection, and the ascension into heaven — these are such deeds, which no how can be explained in a natural way, and is it impossible to be mistaken in such like miracles. This "mistaken explanation" has been cast aside by the unbelievers themselves.

What has been mentioned thus far is not itself the defense of the Gospel, for you must understand that no human fortifications are necessary to the Divine Truth of the Almighty. We have been simply reminded that proofs of the authenticity of the Gospel do exist, and that they are the expression of human thought and energy in man's effort to collect his fellow beings and be at one with Christ and God. Although the Almighty *maketh His angels spirits, and His servants a fiery flame,* yet for our benefit in His love He rewards our efforts with His assistance, and bestows our outreaching arm with the sanctity of Divine authority. It is in this way that we have a most sure defense for Divine things in our human arguments — when they are set forth with love for the salvation of our neighbor.

The proofs of the truthfulness of the Gospel are these: 1. The large number of foretypes in the Old Testament, and the prophecies of the Patriarchs and Prophets during 5,000 years before the birth of our Lord Jesus Christ, both of which are so distinct and connected with historical facts well known to the whole world. These apply directly to the person of Jesus Christ the Messiah and also to our times, i.e. of the New Testament. A careful examination of the proofs under this single head is sufficient to convince a sincere seeker of the truth to embrace the Gospel and become a Christian.

2. Second come the testimonies contained in all the books of the New Testament. Besides the four Evangelists, there were others who labored in putting the Word of God into writing; namely, the Apostles Sts. James, Peter, Jude and Paul. The harmony throughout these Scriptures is indeed marvelous. It is the practiced reader alone who knows how to appreciate the beauty of God's power operating in so many different characters, at different places, in different times and under different circumstances.

3. This proof of the truthfulness of the Gospel is that influence, which only a subjective analysis of the individual life can disclose. You hear it in church in the hymns sung by the choir. Sometimes children see it in the face of their parents and feel it in the presence of their teachers. The penitent criminal speaks of it within the walls of a prison. The Christian soldier glories in it while he falls bleeding. Sometimes the ruler obeys its influence. The mechanic, the merchant likewise pass by its way. The poor widow puts her trust in it when she reads the Bible while surrounded by her hungry children. The dying sleep reposing in the Gospel of Our Lord Jesus Christ.

4. Another proof in defense of our subject is the history of the world. The history of each civilized nation, every legal tribunal of justice, all of the renowned universities of the earth, all of the societies and communities which have a strong hope for ultimate moral progress, the present condition of the family, the advancement of womanhood, the fine critical arguments of the politician, the pride of universal literature, the axiom of science, the investigation of the past, the examination of the present, the cheerful hopefulness of the serious and busy foundation builders of the future, even the glory of music and art, in all this we see traces of the Gospel of Jesus Christ. Moreover it is acknowledged by the world, as plain as black and white, that the teaching of the New Testament is becoming rapidly more and more the inseparable companion to sober, thinking mankind. Thus we have a real objective evidence, moulding history before our very eyes, to the proof of the truthfulness of the Gospel. Long hours of discussion might be devoted to each one of these four witnesses of the Gospel separately. But you cannot bear with them. If I should undertake the gigantic task, I would not be able to finish it.

5. There is yet a fifth argument in favor of Christians. Although the last, it is by no means the least of them. This division contains the testimony of eyewitnesses and their correspondence with contemporaries, and other literary monuments of the first centuries of our era. Upon such important evidence we shall dwell now for a few moments.

In the libraries of Europe, as well as in the libraries of the Eastern Churches, such as Constantinople, Jerusalem, Antioch, Alexandria, Syria, Egypt, Georgia, Armenia, Mt. Athos, Serbia, and also Russia, not a few of the manuscript Gospels of ancient times have been preserved to our day. Some of them belong to the fourth century (i.e. they are almost 1,600 years old). They are the same Gospel that we have today. They describe the same miracles that we know of, and as our sacred scriptures have been copied from these books, so have they been in turn copied from books which were carefully and even jealously guarded — as we learn from immutable history — of the third, then of the second century, and the original books of the holy Apostles and their celebrated companions. The works of the renowned and learned Origen, who wrote his commentaries on the Gospels of Matthew, Luke and John in the third century, and in which the text of the same Gospels is almost completely contained. Origen flourished in the first half of the third century, and besides this, we have the writings of many Fathers of the Church and other Christian workers belonging to the third century, which contain a great many quotations from the Gospels that agree with ours, and concerning the miracles of Jesus Christ. Therefore, there can be no doubt that our Gospel is the same which was read in the third century.

The same must be said of the second half of the second century, after the birth of Christ. We have such works and publications of Fathers and Christian writers belonging to this period, in which we find many places of the Gospels. We will point to the ten books against heresy, which belong to the reverend martyr Irenæus, the Bishop of Lyons. These books were written 150 years after the ascension of our Lord, and the unbelievers themselves do not doubt that Irenæus is the author of them. In these books, there are 400 quotations taken from the four Gospels, and they come in the same order in which we read them today. The texts mentioned refer to the same miracles of Jesus Christ. There are 80 quotations taken from the Gospel of St. John. St. Irenæus speaks of the Evangelists by name, and he gives historical information in regard to the Gospels, which they have written. He affirms that the Church, which was spread widely in his time, held no more nor less than the four Gospels, as there are four sides of the earth, four winds, as the Lord appeared to the Prophet Ezekiel, sitting upon four cherubim. Many places from the Gospels are mentioned also by contemporary writers, such as Tertullian, Clement of Alexandria, and others, so that, upon this literature, which has come down to us from these Christian men of the second half of the second century, and which belongs to them without a doubt, the contents of the four Gospels known to us could be restored. It is acknowledged by students that in the last half of the second century there has been a translation into the Syrian from the

Greek language, not only of the four Gospels, but also of other books of the New Testament known to us.

We have positive witness in the writings of the disciples of the Apostles or their contemporaries, who decidedly ascribe the Gospels to the authorship (of course from the human side) of the Apostles, or to the disciples of the Apostles, as is recognized by the whole Church.

The first witness is St. Polycarp, the reverend martyr, a disciple of St. John the Divine, and other Apostles. He was Bishop of Smyrna in Asia. An epistle of St. Polycarp to the Philippians has been handed down to our day. In it he says: "Anyone who does not confess that Jesus Christ came in the flesh, he is antichrist. In the epistle of John the Apostle and Evangelist, it is said: *Every spirit which confesseth not Jesus Christ as having come in the flesh, the same is not of God, and the same is antichrist.*" Thus, in the first place, this disciple of St. John the Divine speaks of him as the evangelist, consequently John has written the Gospel; and, secondly, to quote literally from the first general epistle of St. John, while this epistle is perfectly alike in style and thought with the fourth Gospel, it is to verify the Apostle John as the writer of this Gospel. We see in the writings of St. Polycarp indications of the Gospel of Matthew and other books of the Apostles. The above-mentioned epistle of St. Polycarp to the Philippians is acknowledged as originally belonging to him by the most reasonable of learned investigators. That St. Polycarp has written this epistle to the Philippians, to this his disciple testified, the above-mentioned reverend martyr Irenæus, and it is difficult to conceive how the genuine epistle of St. Polycarp could have been mutilated or lost and a false one spread abroad in its place. The epistle of St. Polycarp from the time since it was written has been read in the churches of Asia at divine service during the first centuries. It was read even in the fourth century.

Not alone through his writings, but by his long life and his death, which was that of a martyr, does St. Polycarp still more testify to the truth of the Gospel.

By the act of God's providence, not only the Apostle John, but also some of the disciples of the Apostles, lived a long life. St. Irenæus, that great pillar of the structure of proofs, pointing out the original Gospels, testifies that John the Evangelist lived to the time of the Emperor Trajan, who ascended the throne in 98 AD, and died in 117, consequently this Apostle either died in the last two years of the first, or in the beginning of the second century after Christ. This testimony of St. Irenæus, most accurate in itself, as he was the disciple of Polycarp, who was a contemporary and disciple of St. John, yet it is confirmed by many other ancient witnesses, who set the date of the death of John the Divine in the beginning of the second century.

The reverend martyr Polycarp, the disciple of the Apostles, and especially of St. John, lived to be about 110 years. He died in 167 AD. The disciple of Polycarp, St. Irenæus, who was Bishop of Lyons, in the country now called France, was put to death for preaching Christ in 202.

The Gospels of Matthew, Mark and Luke could not be false and appear and be accepted by all the churches before the close of the first century, as some unbelievers say, and likewise the same of the Gospel of John about the year 150, because the immediate disciples of the Apostles would not permit an error, and we know that St. Polycarp was the leader of all the churches in Asia until his martyrdom in 167. It was about 160 AD when Polycarp went to Rome, during the time of Bishop Anecetas, on account of a dispute concerning the time of celebrating Easter (or the Resurrection of our Lord), and therefore, he knew the condition of the churches of the west, as well as of the east. If a difference of time in celebrating Easter Sunday was the cause of such a warm dispute, then what severe quarrels would take place if some of the churches had perchance accepted false gospels.

Yet there is not in all the works of the Fathers and the writers of the second and following centuries so much as the hint of a doubt in the Christian churches, each independent of the other, concerning the authenticity and correctness of the four Gospels. The disciple of Polycarp, St. Irenæus, who had our four Gospels, was also acquainted with the condition of the churches of both the east and west; for in the east he was educated, and in the west he died a bishop. It must be remembered that both men, St. Polycarp and St. Irenæus, ended their life by a martyr's death for preaching Jesus Christ as the Son of God and the Savior of the world. St. Polycarp decided to be burned upon a pile rather than to renounce Christ.

We repeat that St. John the Divine had other disciples, but who of course did not live so long as Polycarp. Nevertheless they could have prevented during the first half of the second century the spreading of any Gospels of Jesus Christ and His miracles, which might not have agreed with the teachings of the Apostles, and particularly of St. John, with whom they have been in close relations. History has deposited for our sake a considerable portion of a letter written by St. Irenæus to his friend, one Florinus, in which he says of a certain heresy: "Thou has not been taught thus by the Presbyters who preceded us, and who listened to the Apostles personally." From this we may conclude that Irenæus and his contemporaries have in their youth studied not alone by St. Polycarp, but also by other disciples of the Apostles.

We may add more facts in connection with the testimony of Irenæus. He was a co-laborer with and in the episcopate a successor of the revered martyr Pothinus, the Bishop of Lyons, in the country of the Gauls, the present France.

Who was St. Pothinus? According to a most ancient tradition of the Church of Lyons, he was a native of Asia, a disciple of Polycarp, and even of the Apostles themselves. In the first half of the second century, he came to Lyons and organized a church, for which he was ordained a bishop. Fifteen years after his arrival in Lyons, upon his request, there were sent to his assistance several men from the east, who were qualified to preach the Gospel, and among whom was the learned St. Irenæus. St. Irenæus became a presbyter in Lyons. In 177, St. Pothinus died in prison during a persecution of the Christians. The year of his death, 177 AD, and his age are clearly certified. In the accounts of this age of martyrs, recorded by an eyewitness and pre-served in the history of Eusebius, it is said of him that he was more that 90 years old at the time of his death. Therefore, they concluded that he was born in 86 AD, and he could have seen the Apostle John. There is no doubt whatever that he was a contemporary, not only of

St. Polycarp, but also of many other apostolic men, who were disciples of St. John the Divine.

He could have known men who have seen other Apostles, that died earlier than St. John, and who labored in preaching the Gospel in Asia, for instance: St. Philip, one of the twelve, who suffered in Hieropolis during the time of the Emperor Domitian (81–96). Thus, Irenæus could have received in Lyons likewise — of St. Pothinus, who was much older than him in age — accurate information concerning the eastern apostolic churches, also of the holy Gospels, and especially of the Gospel of St. John.

Another witness, like St. Polycarp, of the truthfulness of the Gospel is Papius, the Bishop of Hieropolis. He is known as the disciple of the disciples of the Lord. He died about the year 120, earlier than Polycarp. In his work, known as the *Five Books of Explanations of the Words of the Lord*,[2] parts of which are quoted by Eusebius, the historian, he says — on the testimony of the Apostles of Jesus Christ — that the Evangelist Matthew has written the words of the Lord in the Hebrew language, and Mark has written from the dictation of the Apostle Peter of what the Lord did and taught.

Later on another portion of the writings of Papius has been discovered, which proves that he was acquainted with the Gospel of John. Besides this, the historian Eusebius, who had read the writings of Papius, affirms that Papius took as testimony, words from the first epistle of John the Divine; and as this epistle in word and thought is exactly the same as the Gospel of John, it verifies the fact that John was the writer of the Gospel.

A contemporary of Polycarp and other apostolic men was St. Justin, the martyr and philosopher; he was profoundly educated and had written many works, but many of which, unfortunately, have not reached us. Two of his works have come down to us; they are apologies in defense of persecuted Christians, one of which was handed

---

[2] These original documents have been discovered in Mossoul. The Patriarch of Antioch has recently brought them to Paris.

to the Roman Emperor Antoninus Pius about 150 AD, the other after some time was presented to the senate of Rome. The martyr Justin has also put to writing his dialogue with the learned Jew Tryphon in defense of Christianity. What is important for us is the fact that the unbelievers could find nothing to say against the authenticity of the writings of St. Justin, the philosopher, and also the fact that he quotes many places from the Gospels known to us; from the Gospel of Matthew, beginning from the first chapter up to the last, there are fifty quotations; from the Gospel of Luke, about twenty; from the Gospel of John, more than fifteen places, and he also makes mention of another Gospel (i.e. of Mark). He gives the proper name of *evangelia* to the Gospel, and also mentions them *as the remembrances or memory notes of the Apostles and their companions.*

To return again to witness concerning the Evangelist John, it is stated as certain that he spent the last years of his life in Ephesus; here he died and was buried, as Policratus, the Bishop of Ephesus, who lived in the last part of the second century, writes in his letters to Victor, the Bishop of Rome; ancient literature has saved the contents of this letter. Moreover, the Church Universal has always recognized this fact.

As St. Polycarp had for his disciple the reverend-martyr Irenæus, a great witness for the evangelical truth, so had the holy martyr Justin a disciple in the person of Tatian, a witness of the four Gospels. He was a learned pagan, who studied ancient philosophy, but not having found the truth, he turned himself to the Christian Church. He was already a full grown man when he became a pupil of St. Justin in Rome, after which he continued in close friendship with him. After the death of Justin, he went to the east, and in Syria, unfortunately absorbed in meditation, he attached too weighty importance to his own reasoning and fell in heresy. He died about 175 AD. Of his many works there came down to us but one oration, which is lengthy, and it is against the Hellenes or pagans, in defense of Christianity.

What is especially important, Tatian compiled a summary on the ground of the four Gospels, and which he briefly named *Of the Four* (Diatessaron). As this Gospel was compiled literally according to the four Gospels accepted by the Church, it was in use among a considerable portion of Orthodox Christians in the east for a long time for its briefness, and also for less difficult labor in copying, it was preferred to the complete four Gospels. Theodoret, the Bishop of Cyrus, during the first part of the fifth century found more than 200 copies of this Gospel in his diocese. He found nothing in them which did not agree with the universally accepted Gospels, only that Tatian has omitted the genealogy of Jesus Christ and the account of his birth according to the flesh from the seed of David. In its place, Theodoret distributed the original four Gospels, and thereby weakened the memory of Tatian's sad case of heresy.

From all the above-mentioned it is clear that St. Justin, the teacher of Tatian, had accepted the original four Gospels, no more and no less, as the Church at first authorized, including of course the Gospel of St. John. This assertion is strengthened by the canon of New Testament books, which has come down to us, and which has been in use in the Church of Rome during the time of St. Justin. This canon was discovered and published by the learned Muratori. The first part and the end have been lost; it commences thus: "the third book is the Gospel according to Luke." Briefly commenting upon this Gospel, the writer of the canon continues: "the fourth of the Gospels is John's, one of the disciples," and briefly telling about the writing of this Gospel by John the Divine, he goes on, making mention of the book of the "Acts of the Apostles," written by the holy Evangelist Luke. There is no doubt that the first two Gospels in the Roman Church were those of Matthew and Mark, which were known at the close of the first century to the apostolic disciple, Papius, the Bishop of Hieropolis. The Gospel of Mark itself was written by him on the request of the Roman Christians; for this we have the testimony of St. Clement of Alexandria, a learned man of the second century; a proof of this is also the Gospel itself, which contains a considerable number of Roman words.

Soon after the death of Pius the first, during the time of his successor, Bishop Anecetas, about 160 AD, as we have mentioned before, the aged Polycarp, the Bishop of Smyrna, a disciple of St. John and other Apostles, came to Rome on account of a dispute concerning the time of celebrating the day of the Resurrection of our Lord, which had arisen between the churches. And, of course, it was necessary to turn to the Gospels while speaking about this subject. If the Gospel of St. John, undoubtedly held by the Roman Church at the time, was not authentic, St. Polycarp would surely bring the case forward, and a dispute would have arisen concerning this Gospel, or the Roman Church would have excluded it from the list of New Testament books, but there was no such proceeding; consequently, the Gospel of John belonged to the Apostle himself.

It must be taken into consideration that in all the works of the apostolical men and other writers of the first and the earlier part of the second century there is expressed a clear faith in Jesus Christ, as the Son of God, who was incarnate of the Most Holy Virgin on earth, who worked great signs and miracles, who arose from the dead and ascended into heaven, and it is also clearly shown that the Christians of this period had known none other Christ, but Him who is revealed in the Gospel.

No less important for the proof of our subject, at least for these careful treasurers of the truth in the early centuries, is the example of holy life and also the tradition of the very first Christians, of whom there were more than 500 that had seen Jesus Christ. It was but the tenth day after our Lord had ascended into heaven, and when He sent down upon the Church power from the Almighty, that over three thousand more were added to the followers of Him, whom great multitudes of people on many occasions followed when He walked upon earth with His twelve, who were themselves in their first simplicity rather skeptical believers of only the real — which could be seen with the eyes and felt with the hands.

I hope you will bear cheerfully a moment or two longer, while we bring these testimonies of ancient literature to a close. Yet, I must admit, it has been for your sakes, that this subject is considerably abridged.

About 130 AD the holy martyr Codratus, who was Bishop in Magnesia, was put to death for his faith in Christ. He was a disciple of the Apostles and a prophet. The reverend-martyr Codratus is known for his writing which he handed to the Roman Emperor Adrian in 126, in defense of the persecuted Christians. Although this apology has not reached our times, yet it was read by Eusebius the historian, who quotes from it the following: "The works of our Savior (writes Codratus to the Emperor) have always been manifest, because they were truthful. Those whom He healed and resurrected from the dead were visible — not only when He healed and resurrected them, but always. They lived not only during His life on earth, but remained considerably longer after He left us; some of them have lived to our day," i.e. to the time between 80–90 AD, when Codratus was in the prime of life

In support of this investigation, we bring forward historical facts, and when such come from heretics or even unbelievers, they are the more valuable, as the work is shown thereby to be impartial, and the Divine to be above the need of a human justification.

Thus, another heretic, Valentine by name, boasted that he had received his teaching from Theodala, a disciple of the Apostle Paul. Valentine preached in Egypt between 120–130. He settled in Rome about 140 AD. According to the testimony of Irenæus and Tertullian, writers of the second century, Valentine had made use of the whole of Sacred Scriptures. In the book of St. Irenæus against heresy, not only many parts of the Gospels are mentioned, but also quotations from the holy Apostle Paul, which were perverted by the unorthodox explanations of the Valentinians. The reverend-martyr Hippolytus ascribes to Valentine these words: "all the prophets and the law speak through Demiurgus, the god of non-reason." Therefore, the Savior saith: *"all who came before Me, the same were thieves and outlaws."* Now this text is found only in the Gospel of St. John. It is known also that Heracleon, a disciple of Valentine, had written a commentary on the Gospel of John, considerable parts of which have been preserved in Origen's commentary on the Gospels. Heretics, as well as others, who lived in the second century, would not have accepted of the Church the Gospel, moreover a false one, if their founders and teachers who lived in the time of the apostlic men were not firmly convinced of its authenticity. St. Irenæus, in the second half of the second century, wrote thus: "*Our Gospels are strongly established,*" even heretics become their witness; quoting from which they expect to uphold their doctrine. Heresy, which began to show itself so early among Christians, was the cause nevertheless why the first bishops and other leaders of the churches kept so diligent a watch over the Gospels in their original completeness, and guarded them from any and all mutilation, which some of the heretics attempted, but of which they were accused in good season.

Only recently, in a responsible magazine published in the eastern metropolis of America, October 28, 1899, the profoundly learned Professor William C. Winslow, D.D., D.C.L., L.L.D. writes: "Among the papyri discovered at Behnesa by the Egypt Exploration Fund is a fragment of the Gospel of St. John, which proves to be of the highest importance and deepest interest. It antedates all our previously known texts by one hundred years or more. Our associates have now completed their critical study of the text, and a facsimile of it will appear in our volume about ready for the press, with a great many documents of the first century translated. The papyrus of the first chapter of St. Matthew (AD 150), corroborating our version of St. Matthew 1:18–21, and the Logia (New Sayings of Christ) were in book form. This fragment of St. John is also in book form.

It has been assumed that the form of writing in a book or codex dated from the introduction of vellum; but the foregoing and like discoveries by the Fund show that such fashion was in use for Christian literature of the earliest times.

The St. Matthew and Logia fragments are in single leaves, but the papyrus of St. John is on a sheet, and is written upon both sides. Moreover, the first leaf contains St. John 1, and the second leaf St. John 20 in part; so that we possess one of the outer sheets of a large quire between which and chapter 20 were the intervening eighteen chapters, now lost. This book of the Gospel contained about fifty pages.

It is to be noted that the usual contractions for theological words like God, Jesus, Christ, and Spirit are used. If such contractions were familiar in the second century, they must have been introduced much earlier. Do they not show the existence of a Christian literature as early as 100 AD?

The text, a small uncial, resembles that of the Codex Sinaiticus, to which variants of its own are added. But the facsimile will reveal this and other characteristics to the scholar who sees our coming volume, and the Christian public will be deeply interested in the publication of a text containing the statement, '*The Word Was Made Flesh,*' which words were accepted in the early morning of Christianity as very truth. *Out of Egypt have I called my Son* may be transliterated for to-day: 'Out of Egypt comes the proofs for the Bible as God's revelation to man.'"

Christianity is not so much in danger of a so-called "learned unbelief," as it is of the "little faith" and practical unbelief in active life, and the spreading of unchristian habits and customs, and in danger from the life even of Christians, which is not according to the Gospel. Many, Oh many so-called Christians of our times are in need of having their hearts renewed, and deeply impressed with the words of the Savior "*repent and believe in the Gospel.*"

The True Church of Christ[3]

Wwhat is the Orthodox Church? The Orthodox Church is a body or community of people, who, 1 — correctly believe in divine revelation; and 2 — who obey a lawful hierarchy instituted by our Lord Jesus Christ Himself, through the holy Apostles. In order to belong to the Orthodox Church, two principal conditions are required: First — to accurately accept, rightly understand and truthfully confess the divine teaching of faith; and secondly — to acknowledge the lawful hierarchy or priesthood, to receive from it the holy mysteries or sacraments, and generally to follow its precepts in matters concerning salvation.

Let us now consider the question concerning the true and divine doctrine of holy faith.

The divine teaching of our holy religion is contained in the books of the holy Scriptures of the Old and the New Testaments, and in holy Tradition. The principal dogma (these truths), i.e. the sacramental ones (which may also be understood as the theoretical), are laid down briefly in the "creed," which commences with these words: *I believe in one God, the Father,* and which was compiled by the holy Fathers of the first two universal councils in the fourth century. The moral truths of the Orthodox Faith are contained chiefly in the Ten Commandments given by God to Moses on Mt. Sinai which were

---

[3] The author is indebted for assistance in compiling the purely theological portions of these papers to the works of the M. Rev. Dr. Sergius, Archbishop of Vladimir, Russia.

completed and explained by our Lord Jesus Christ in the Gospel and especially in the Lord's Sermon on the Mount.

The doctrine, which does not agree with the true understanding of holy Scripture and holy tradition, which is preserved in the Orthodox Catholic Church from the Apostles' time, is termed heresy; translated from the Greek language, this word signifies separation. Certainly it is to be understood that such who separate or draw others away from the body of the Church by false teaching, thereby they excommunicate themselves from her fold.

Heresy, or injury to the teaching of Christ, has begun as early as the times of the Apostles. St. Paul wrote to Titus, who was bishop on the island of Crete: "A man that is a heretic after a first and second admonition refuse, knowing that such a one is perverted, and sinneth, being self-condemned" (Titus 3:10, 11). The holy Apostle Paul has written to the Corinthian Christians thus: "For there must be also heresies among you, that they which are approved may be made manifest among you" (1 Cor. 9:19). The bishops, as the successors of the Apostles, endeavored from the earliest times to transmit the teaching of Christ, which they received from the Apostles accurately. Thus our faith was carefully, even to the letter, transmitted by tradition. It is plainly understood how holy tradition became a channel by which truths were conveyed to rising generations, as the first bishops themselves received the word and also necessary instructions from the Apostles, not only in writing, but also orally; i.e. by word, face to face; therefore, it is clear that this apostolic tradition was in itself an explanation of the holy Scriptures, as it were — a supplement. In regard to holy writ, the bishops were careful that no false books be counted in with the genuine collection, which was left by the Apostles, and also that the original writings of the Apostles themselves be not injured or marred by heretics through the least addition or omission to the text of holy Scripture. And if a false teacher be found, his teachings were at once examined by the bishops, and they declared before the Church universal that such and such a doctrine was not known to them, that they did not receive it from the Apostles, and that it did not agree with the doctrine of the Apostles. Heresy caused the gathering of local and general councils, in which the false teaching was compared with the holy Scripture and tradition and then rejected. In course of time the apostolic tradition, which was transmitted orally at first, was gradually, as the necessities of the Church demanded, committed to writing; and it is found in the works of the holy Fathers and teachers of the first several centuries.

Although all heretics, whoever they be, do not belong to the Church, yet, judging from the character of their false teaching, some are nearer to her, while others are greatly separated from her, and therefore, the Church receives into her communion the repentant heretics differently; namely — by three distinct offices during public worship. These offices were formulated in the time of the general councils. If we are spared, we shall in some future time explain these offices, and also what differences and contradictions there are in the heresies themselves. Now we continue to briefly review the Orthodox Faith.

The principal dogma of our religion are these: 1 — The doctrine of God as He is in His being; one God in substance, but in three persons; the Trinity consubstantial and undivided; the Father unoriginate; the Son begotten of the Father before all ages; and the Holy Spirit, who proceeds from the Father. 2 — The doctrine of the Son of God, as the Savior of the human race; the second person of the Most Holy Trinity, the Son of God, who was incarnate for our salvation of the Most Holy Virgin Mary, who suffered and died in the flesh, arose again; ascended into the heavens, and He shall come again to judge the living and the dead. 3 — The doctrine of the Holy Spirit, as the sanctifier and perfecter of the salvation of mankind; that He is sent on earth by the Father for the merits of Jesus Christ, and abides in the holy, catholic and apostolic Church, preserves in her the orthodox teaching of faith unimpaired and saves the faithful chiefly by means of the holy mysteries (or sacraments), regenerating, enlightening, edifying and strengthening in the spiritual life. Upon these truths are founded also the other dogma of the Christian religion; viz: That of the Mother of God,[4] the veneration of the saints of God, sacred images, the administration of the Church, etc.

We have already learned that the true confession of faith by itself is not sufficient for salvation. Of necessity another condition is required to belong to the Orthodox Church, and that is the recognition of a lawful hierarchy (or priesthood), the reception of sacraments from the same hierarchy, and obedience to it in matters concerning salvation. In a community of Christians in which there is no lawful bishop, who is the dispenser of the gifts of saving grace, there are no sacramental gifts of the Holy Spirit, there can be no mystery of the body and blood of Christ, and where the Holy Spirit and Christ are not present, who sacramentally abide in Christians, there, of course, can be no Church. Sacred Scripture testifies to this very decidedly.

Let us turn our attention to the eighth chapter of the Acts of the Apostles. What do we read there? At the time when a great persecution arose against the Church in Jerusalem and the holy archdeacon Stephen was stoned to death, then the Christians, excepting the Apostles, scattered in different places of Judea and Samaria. The deacon Philip, who came into the city of Samaria, preached Christ there. The people with one heart gave heed to what Philip said, seeing the miracles which he worked; for the unclean spirits came out of many; some they left with wild cries, and many who were impotent and lamed became whole. And there was great joy in that city. There was a man in that place, one Simon by name, who before this practiced sorcery and confounded the people of Samaria, giving himself out as someone great. Many followed him, saying that he had the power of God. But when they believed Philip, who spoke to them of the good tidings of the kingdom of God and of the name of Jesus Christ, they received baptism of him, both men and women. And so did Simon believe, and after being baptized he remained with Philip, and, seeing the great powers and signs which were manifested, he wondered. The Apostles, who were in Jerusalem, having heard that Samaria received

---

[4] See the author's *Ritual, Services and Sacraments of the Eastern Apostolic Church.*

the word of God, sent to them Peter and John, who, having come, prayed over them that they might receive the Holy Spirit, and laying their hands upon them they received the Holy Spirit. Upon seeing that, by the laying on of the Apostles' hands, the Holy Spirit was given, Simon brought them money, saying: Give me this power, that upon whomsever I lay my hands the same will receive the Holy Spirit. But Peter said unto him: Thy silver perish with thee, because thou hast thought to obtain the gift of God with money. Thou has neither part nor lot in this matter.

From this history it can be seen that during the time of the Apostles, there were grades in the hierarchy. Philip, who was one of the seven deacons, notwithstanding that he received grace for the office of a deacon from the Apostles, notwithstanding that by the Holy Spirit, who was with him, he performed many great works, yet he could not bring down the Holy Spirit upon the Samaritans, whom he had baptized. But when the Apostles Peter and John had come, they prayed and laid their hands upon them. Then the Holy Spirit came down upon them and was manifested in signs and miracles. The Apostles transmitted the power of conferring the Holy Spirit only to the bishops. In other parts of the same book of the Acts of the Apostles, and in the epistles of St. Paul to Timothy, the Bishop of Ephesus, and to Titus, the Bishop of Crete, there are plain statements pertaining to the grade or office of presbyter, which is a middle one, between the episcopate and diaconate.

Which hierarchy is the true and lawful one? It is the priesthood which had retained, and continued to follow these conditions.

1 — In the first place such a hierarchy is true, which received the grace of the Holy Spirit from the Apostles themselves in an unbroken line of succession from one to another. If, for instance, in a certain locality the bishops and priests were found to be wanting, the succession being broken, and in their absence the laity elected new ones and lay their hands upon them, and proclaimed them to be bishops and presbyters, such a hierarchy would be unlawful and without grace, as the laity cannot transmit that which they do not possess

themselves—the grace of the priesthood. In the time when the erring Church of Rome was the cause of the Protestant separation in the sixteenth century, there was not a bishop in any of the countries that sided with them, excepting in England alone,[5] where Protestantism appeared later than in Germany. The Protestants commenced to elect and establish presbyters themselves, and these ministers not only baptize, but they officiate at a so-called communion service, which of course is not a valid sacrament, as the ministers have no apostolic ordination, and they are not presbyters.

As we learn from history, it is only such a hierarchy which is authentic—that received the grace of the priesthood from the Lord Jesus Christ's Apostles themselves, through an unbroken succession of the lawful heirs of this sacrament. And this is necessary. As the inclination to sin is transmitted successively from one to another by inheritance in the conception and birth of the body, thus also grace, that is the power of God, which wipes away sin and gives strength in struggle with it, for the merits of the new Adam, the Lord Jesus Christ, being bestowed, it is transmitted uninterruptedly by the laying on of episcopal hands in the priesthood, by anointing all Christians with holy chrism, and also through sacred acts and visible forms in other sacraments.

2. Secondly, an authentic hierarchy is such, which confesses all the truths of holy religion, for there are heresies which entirely deprive bishops and priests of the ministerial grace.

3. Thirdly, a priesthood to be lawful must administer the sacraments orderly, according to the rules of the holy catholic Church, not changing essential actions, as there are acts and conditions in the rites of mysteries that are essential, without which a certain sacrament may not be valid. Should a sacred minister violate an essential rule he is subject to degradation, if the violation has been intentional, or, at least, the mystery is void of power. The seventh rule of the apos-

---

[5] Individually, we have not the power to assert that the Church of England has retained all the conditions whereby she may not be an erring branch of the Catholic Church.

tolic canon enjoins: "Should anyone, bishop or presbyter, administer not three immersions in baptism in commemoration of the death of the Lord, but one, let him be cast out." And those who were baptized by one immersion, it was ordered that they should be rebaptized. If a priest should consecrate chrism himself, and anoint the newly baptized with it, such an act would not be the mystery of unction with chrism, because it would be the usurpation of the rights and the power of a bishop, and such a thing is forbidden presbyters by the sixth rule of the Council of Carthage. Should a bishop or priests use only water in place of wine in the mystery of communion, as some heretics do, such an offering would not be a true sacrament.

4. Fourthly, to be a lawful and true hierarchy the same must be governed and must govern its spiritual charge according to the rules of the holy Apostles, the seven Ecumenical Councils and other laws which are accepted by the Orthodox Church in general. Having apostatized from these universal or catholic Church regulations, the Roman Church invented a doctrine concerning the supremacy of the Bishop of Rome over all the Christian churches. This has been one of the chief causes of the Romish schism or separation from the Orthodox Catholic Church.

5. A fifth condition necessary for proving the lawfulness of the priesthood is its unity with the Orthodox Church in the spirit of peace and love. Whoever destroys the unity, except for a genuine and important cause, and the bishops and priests together with Christians who follow them, that separate themselves from the higher Church authorities, are excommunicated from the Church, according to the rules of the Apostles and the canons of the councils.

The Orthodox Church, which is one, is one spiritual body, animated only by the Holy Spirit, having only one head — the Lord Jesus Christ.

The Orthodox Church is holy, not having spot or wrinkle or any such thing (Ephes. 5:27). She sanctifies sinners by her teaching and sacraments.

The Orthodox Church is Catholic, i.e. collective, because she was organized by the Lord Jesus Christ for the salvation of all people in the whole world, and she is the gathering of all true believers in all places, times and peoples.

The Orthodox Church will continue on earth until the second coming of Christ, *imperishable and not conquered by any powers of hell.* In regard to holy doctrine, she is blameless and will ever remain unchangeable, as she has abiding in her the Holy Spirit, the spirit of truth, therefore she is, according to the Apostle, *a pillar and the foundation of truth* (1 Tim. 3:15). The existence of the lawful hierarchy and the administration of the holy mysteries will never cease in the Church.

The Lord Jesus Christ Himself had said: *I will build My Church, and the gates of hell will not prevail against her,* and again: *Behold I am with you always, even unto the end of ages.* Therefore, it is the duty of the Christian to obey the Church, for, outside of her, there is no salvation. *If thy brother neglect to hear the Church, let him be to thee as an heathen man and a publican* (Matt. 18:17), saith the Lord.

May God, who is glorified in the Trinity, help us by His grace to become, through our membership in the Church Militant on earth, members of the Church Triumphant in heaven, that we may glorify His all-honorable and majestic name with the angels and saints forever, without end. Amen.

The Education of Children

We desire to tell you of something, which is of the utmost importance. We find it necessary, unfortunately, to repeat in a measure what has been told you several times. We speak plainly, without a flourish of words, because we feel our responsibility before God — if we be misunderstood. We desire to remind you of our parish or church-school. To learn to read and write you send your children to school. You know that you must do it. But how many of you think of the serious obligation of *rightly* and thoroughly preparing your children for the *life* which they must live after only a few years? Some, indeed, give their attention to what they call a decent education for their children, for which and for whom they would not fall back of anyone, but be as good and as nice as other people in town. If you send your children to school to study grammar and arithmetic (the future mainstay of the "home" are often compelled to leave their homes to learn even cooking and dancing), why will you not be just as eager to send them to school where they will study religion? If you are truly interested in the welfare of your children, why do you not watch as strictly, but once a week, how they attend to their lessons in the study of the Law of God, as you do in some homework, which the children seemed to be forced to have prepared within the next twelve hours for their public school? You must obey God, above the public and all other masters, or lose your souls for the responsibility which rests upon you for the present and future welfare of your children.

Where there is intellect, there always will be knowledge. Still, you must educate the child. Teach the boy and girl geography and history; but if you do not train the child's will, in order not only to please you, its parents, but to bend before the holy will of Him, who is the only just rewarder of good and evil, then you are a failure as a Christian. Where there is no discipline, there is no constancy. Where there is no law, there is no order, no peace, no everlasting happiness. If no tender sympathies re-echo in the heart of the young, away have been cast the time and labor in teaching — be it botany or music.

What a pity! We see young children at the age of ten, whose very brains seem to be rattling with numerical problems, while they have not the good manners to step out of the way of an old person, or even the common human feeling of a desire to aid in distress. I have seen even young men and young women stand gazing on one of their company, who was fainting from exhaustion, without the offer of the most simple service — to fetch a cup of cold water.

However, regular athletic exercises are attended to, no matter how carefully the lessons in physiology are prepared, little indeed, will they profit your children, if they know not the steps, up which they must climb to seek the *Highest*. If you, fathers and mothers, are Christians, then we *ministers of the Word* may rest in the quiet hope that your children have been taught dutifully and rightly to praise the All-majestic Creator at morn, likewise in midday, *confessing each themselves before God, and openly before all men, confessing God,* while at night they humbly implore His mercy. But if your children do not invoke their Guardian-Angel, if they do not bless the most pure Mother of our Lord Jesus Christ, and fall down in humble devotion, supplicating for the grace of our Heavenly Father, then you are not Christians.

It is a sad fact, which must be recorded in this earthly judgment seat of God, and the truth of this fact is as bitter for me, as it is for you. Nevertheless, we acknowledge and accept the truthful bitterness with the hope that it will prove to be a healing remedy, which will bring peaceful and sweet results.

There are parents belonging to our congregation in San Francisco, who go to the matinee with their children, not giving a thought before hand to the character of the play; they teach the little ladies and gentlemen, i.e. the future men and women of a Christian land, to buy and select wearing apparel, which is pleasing to the eyes of the world, whether it be healthful and sensible, or not. Yes, they are "up to the times," they visit the classes of the public schools; they receive and fix their signatures to monthly school reports. Ah! If they would but fix the character of the school itself. If their children are tardy for five minutes they may not go to school without a written excuse. Yet it is in the power of the citizens of this country to have laws enacted, which would protect their young from being crammed with "ologies" and "isms," and ensure their healthful growth and the teaching of good sense.

How is it with our church schools? All our children do not attend, and their friends and Christian neighbors do not take interest enough to invite them to go with their children. The parents do not visit our school, but once a year, and then — when we are not at work. What is our homework for the children? Only a little of that which is the greatest. A very little, once or twice a week, of the commandments of God and the Gospel of His Son, Jesus Christ. And no one to think about it; no one at home to see that the life-work of the family is done! During the short hour that we manage to collect a few unruly children, we must study and repeat, for even prayers are not learned in the home.

Beloved Christians! We need your cooperation. We may sow the seed, but — remember — the influence of your home is the sunshine which heats the ground. So then ask yourselves, is not the wind too chilly, and the sun too low to strike its rays direct? We may trim the plant, but it is your duty to keep watering it. Oh! If you would but water the precious plants of your gardens with prayerful tears! We invite you to visit our school, from time to time, during lesson hours. If we were asked, how many of us pray together with children, the conscientious would answer, a very, very few; only several in a congregation of three hundred souls. Generally, of an evening, the children are sent to bed; and sometimes someone calls out, say your prayers first. And from time to time there is a prayer, but more often there is only the "saying." Must I explain that Christian children should be followed to their night's rest; in most cases they should be "put" into bed.

It is the duty especially of parents to see that their children pray correctly, and also to pray with them in an audible voice themselves. Let this not be an act of routine. Do not for a moment think that it will become a daily routine. This reasonable discipline, when you kneel by the side of tender childhood and see the little ones pray, will lighten in your own heart — at the same time that it does in theirs — the fire of heavenly love. Moreover, your prayers must be the prayers of the Orthodox Church of Christ. Our Mother Church has but one infallible model of prayer — given to her by our Lord Jesus Christ. It is an invocation, petitions, and a doxology; in other words, a call, a request, and a praise. If you will concentrate your minds upon the subject of each one of these divisions, then your prayer will not be a "saying," but an "offering." Again we ask you to give us your dutiful attention and assistance in the work of teaching our children. If not for the sake of your own comfort in old age and sickness, let us for the sake of their Almighty Father in Heaven, and our Judge, awaken in their hearts the love for that which is holy and truly beautiful. Amen.

Sermon on New Year's Day

Thy Kingdom Come (Matt. 6:10)

The first day of a new year may not be kept as a holy day and a day of quiet by everyone, as the Church enjoins that it should be, yet it is a day, nevertheless, peculiarly distinguished from other days by every thinking man and woman. New Year's Day is looked upon by some with that awe, which is always respectful before the mysterious. For some it has a strong fascination, which is expressed in their holiday-making, often bordering on senseless hilarity. For others it is a short day into which they vainly strive to encompass eternity, or even the one year which it represents.

The merry callers, together with the pleasant entertainers, and the busy crowd of elders, together with the happy ones of new and young fortune, cannot hide from us even on New Year's Day in the great congregation of humankind those faces that look on us with serious mien, those eyes of careful thought, that wistful gaze of longing, those eyes that burn with a desire. Some of these last named are those who were, so to illustrate, moulded into an image of melancholy composure, whom painful anxiety could not conquer and make of their rich natures absolute pessimists, by robbing them of their last hope; and some are those who have force, power, hidden away down in their souls, who persevere, quietly abiding their time, when they may openly and fully cherish their own desires, satisfy their secret aspirations, and gain the end of their passion — strong ambition. Some again are the ones who very nicely *put on their back the sheep's skin, but inwardly they are the ferocious wolf.* They take you with their soft hand, but nothing is left you; sweetly they look upon you with quiet eyes, but you find yourself to be lost; they kiss you, and you are betrayed by Judas. Still we find among the last mentioned, i.e. of those with serious and longing mien, such characters as cannot be influenced aside from the path they chose for their life walk, either by wealth or by social happiness, nor can poverty or misery eat and destroy their individuality. Fame, position, science, art, comfort and society's opinion call out to them: *To you will I give all this authority, and the glory of them … if you will but worship me, it shall be yours.* No, to the mighty ones of this world answer they; is it right to hearken unto you, rather than unto God? This little flock of the chosen ones go steadily along the narrow path. Praising the Almighty Creator, they draw near, and before the awful presence of the Supreme Being, they pray; without condemnation and with boldness, they dare to say: *Father, our Father, who art in heaven! hallowed be Thy name, Thy kingdom come, preserve us from the taint of the world*, so that the evil spirit with his passions and servants may not rule over us; teach us to worship Thee in the spirit and in the truth, so that the changing etiquette of a vanishing sphere, and the vain philosophy of time servers may not harm nor forbid us to call to Thee: "Lord, Thy kingdom come."

"I wish you a happy new year." Such is the universal greeting on this day among friends. Man salutes man on the first day of a new year and expresses the hope that the new year may be a happy one for each. Ah! and so it is happiness, the aim and end of all, which is the one thing most desired. That is what Christians ask for when they pray to God: *Thy kingdom come.* And it is just for this purpose that this altar was built for us. That was the desire of our fathers, who contemplated over thirty years ago to organize a parish and have a house of prayer in this city, and which they realized, thanks to the Christian sympathy of the Holy Synod of the Russian Church.

Happiness — that was the mission object of the Apostles, who walked the earth. It as for our happiness that Jesus Christ came and commenced for the whole world and all time a new and everlasting year. Did not even the heavens and their spiritual ministers proclaim it? Yea, face to face and heart in heart, did Mary encompass it. To Joseph it was in a dream. It was gloriously indicated to the learned magicians by a moving star. But for the peasant on the fields the angels sang. Yes, for this gift to humankind, for this happiness of the new year to the world the spiritual powers of heaven thanked the Lord. They sang: *Glory to God in the Highest, and on earth peace, good will toward men.*

As we today commence another period by which we measure that which we call time, and as we feel that this time is gliding past us, flowing swifting beyond our reach, and stripping us, too, of that which we sometimes think belongs to our person, we surely ought give serious thought to the one thing so needful, to the happiness we wish our friends from year to year, to the great boon our spirits yearn for, even though it be on our part sometimes unknowingly. Let us renew within us the faculties of our soul, so overburdened with a generally prevailing materialism. Let us renew within us our hearts, and prepare a clean habitation for this great gift. Let us strengthen our desire, once elevated, and let us reach out, and accept, and follow this great happiness of God in man! O God, save us from the rule which our own severally different, irreligious and selfish opinions create, and from the kingdom of darkness, and let *Thy kingdom come!*

It is often just so with the life of a man as the traveler of great deserts experiences. He now is under the hot sun with no water, and then the cold atmosphere of the night finds him without a roof. With sore foot and tired eye he goes along until he comes to an oasis; the fresh scene dispels the monotony; his heavy heart is gladdened. Such an oasis we find even in the barren hearts of all men of the world; but not so often, not so fruitful and so refreshing as in the life of an humble and obedient believer in the Allguiding Providence of God. Oh, Christians! Watch for those bright moments in your life. Prosper in the real happiness and shine forth in the darkness of a sinful world — a light to others. Stop on these green and fresh pastures. Rest. Look over the past and examine the way. Consider the different kinds of temptations you underwent. Know thyself; where were you the weakest? Which place on the road was it the most difficult to pass? How have you come out of the battle? What is it you have lost? Did you gain anything? If so, is it good for your salvation? Can your neighbor profit by it?

Let us hear Solomon, the wisest of all earthly born, the richest and greatest king of his time; let us hear what he says in one of those bright moments of his life, when he was most fit and capable to rightly diagnose his self-examination. He says: "*I have seen all the works that are done under the sun; and, behold, all is vanity and vexation of Spirit. I communed with my own heart, saying, Lo, I am come unto great estate, and have gotten more wisdom than all they that have been before me in Jerusalem; yea, my heart hath great experience of wisdom and knowledge. And I gave my heart to know wisdom, and to know madness, and folly: I perceived that this also is vexation of spirit. I made me great works, I builded me houses, I planted me vineyards. All kinds of trees and flowers I had in my gardens. I made me pools of water. I got me servants and maid servants. I gathered me also silver and gold. I was great. Also my wisdom remained with me. Then I looked on all the works that my hands had wrought, and on the labor that I had labored to do, and, behold, all was vanity and vexation of spirit, and there was no profit under the sun* * * ** When we read farther on and come to the close of Solomon's repentant confession, he says: "*Let us hear the conclusion of the whole matter, fear God and keep His commandments, for this is the whole duty of man. For God shall bring every work into judgment, with every secret thing, whether it be good, or whether it be evil.*"

On this New Year's Day, when we look over the past and see our mistakes, our weakness, our folly, and our sins, and when from today we look to the future with renewed hope, wishing as much as ever before — a happy new year, our good resolutions must be carried out with a strong will. When we learn to seek our happiness in that *one thing above all needful*; when we learn to bend our wills to the pleasures of that Supreme Will, which rules all, then we will have found *the good portion, which shall not be taken away from us.* The Kingdom of God will have come.

But to some I know this appears to be a hard saying. It is well to *talk* about such high things, but how can we *practice* a heavenly life upon earth, they question. Certainly the thought about earthly things is indispensable to our earthly life. Do but observe how we abandon things heavenly, for things earthly, and we shall find it not so difficult to put aside earthly things for things heavenly. We limit the time we employ in works of charity and religious practice, in order to have more time for worldly things. Sometimes we go into the Church of God, and at the same time we are thinking of that which engages our minds at home and at our business. And sometimes, even, while standing bodily in the house of prayer, our thoughts are attracted elsewhere, by our worldly affections, or by the passions which rule in us; even the very prayer of some is tainted by flitting worldly thoughts! Now do the very reverse. Do that which is necessary for your earthly existence, but endeavor not to extend it beyond the necessary, and strive to liberate yourself as much as possible from such labor, in order to have more time and freedom for works of piety. Restrain your thoughts from earthly things, not only when standing before God in His temple, but wherever you may be, when obliged to busy yourself with earthly things, occasionally turn away your thoughts and especially your desires for them, and lift up your heart unto heaven and God. When you set about worldly affairs, remember God, and ask for His blessing and assistance; when you go to rest, remember God and give thanks unto Him for His assistance in your labors, and for the gift of rest.

Thus we may unite every earthly work, not contrary to the law of God, with a love of things above, and, so to say, change earthly and visible things, into things heavenly and spiritual. When thou lookest upon the sun, said once a saint, seek the true sun, for thou art blind. When thou turnest thy gaze upon light, turn towards thy soul, and see whether thou hast there the true and blessed light, which is the Lord.

May the light of our Lord Jesus Christ illumine, may His Spirit strengthen each of us, and may our walking according to His Word and His Life, lead us all here upon earth to set our affections on things above, and thereby conduct us to the blessed contemplation of Him in heaven, where reigneth supreme the happiness of all sincere seekers of the true new year. Amen.

Thoughts on Fast
and Temperance

Man, having received his present being, consisting of a visible body and intellectual, immaterial soul, is a complex being. But the nature and worth of both the just named parts are not of equal value. The body is made as an instrument that is moved by the order of a ruler; the soul is designed to govern and command it, as the superior of an inferior. The soul, receiving from the intellect and reason the means by which it makes distinctions, may, possessing such a quality of distinction, separate the truly beautiful from its common imitation; it may perceive God as the Creator and Designer, not only of that which is underneath our feet and received by our senses, but that, also, which is hidden from the eyes, and of which the immaterial mind may contemplate, having the power of imagination at its command.

Practicing, as the godly one, in righteousness and virtue, she aspires unto divine wisdom, and, obeying its laws and commands, withdraws as much as possible from the desires of the flesh, comes nearer to God, and strives by all its strength to ally itself with the good. The particular and most important object of this sacred philosophy is temperance; as it is the mind, which is not disturbed, but free of all influences of pollution, arising from the stomach or other senses, that has a continual action and contemplates the heavenly, the things pertaining to its own sphere.

And so it behooves us, the lovers of all things pure, the lovers of the word of God, yea — even Christians, to love the present time, which our holy Church has set apart for a special opportunity of obtaining greater grace in the sight of God. We should hail with joy such an opportunity! The time I refer to is the Advent Lent. We should love this fast as the teacher of sobriety, the mother of virtue, the educator of the children of God, the guardian of the unruly, the quiet of the soul, the staff of life, the peace that is firm and serene. Its importance and strictness pacifies the passions, puts out the fire of anger and wrath, cools and quiets the agitation produced by over-eating. And, as in summer time, when the sweltering heat of the sun hangs over the ground, the northern breeze proves a blessing to the sufferers, scattering the closeness by its pleasant coolness, so does likewise fast, destroying the overabundance of heat in the body, which is caused by gluttony. Proving to be of so much benefit to the soul. Lent brings the body no less benefit. It refines the coarseness of matter, releases the body of part of its burden, lightens the blood vessels that are often ready to burst with an overflow of blood, and prevents them becoming clogged, which may happen as easily as it occurs with a water pipe, that, when being forced to maintain the abundance of water pressed into it by a powerful machine, bursts from the pressure. And the head feels light and clear when the blood-vessels do not nervously beat, and the brain does not become clouded by the spreading of evaporations. Abstinence gives the stomach ease, which relieves it from a forced condition of slavery, and from boiling like a boiler, working with a sickly effort to cook the food it contains. The eyes look clear and undimmed, without the haze that generally shadows the vision of a glutton. The activity of the limbs is stable, that of the hand firm; the breath is regular and even, and not burdened by pent-up organs. The speech of him who fasts is plain and distinct; the mind is pure, and then it is that the mind shows forth its true image of God, when, as if in an immaterial body, it quietly and undisturbedly exercises the functions belonging to it. The sleep is quiet and free from all apparitions. Not to extend unnecessarily, we may sum up by saying that fast is the common peace of the soul and body. Such are the beneficent results of a temperate life; and such are the precepts of a Christian life. It is a law of the Holy Church, which prescribes that we should fast during the Lenten season.

Do you not know that angels are the constant watchers and guardians of those that fast, just as the demons, those very friends of greasy stuffs, those lovers of blood and companions of drunkards, are the associates of those that give themselves up to debauchery and orgies during such a holy time as Lent. The angels and saints, as also the evil spirits, ally themselves with those they love, they become related with that, which is pleasing to them. Every day in our life God points out a lesson to us concerning the eternal life, but we very seldom heed it; in a word, we generally don't care! Oh, is this not terrible to think of? And yet no one man will deliberately, so to speak, attempt to slight the Almighty Creator, no one who is capable of using his understanding in the very least degree. But yet, beloved brethren, we do it! We, day after day, in our worldly habits unconsciously say: "I don't care!" Have we a right to do anything at all unconsciously, when He, in whose hand the very breath of our life flutters as a very weak, little thing, when He, I say, bestowed upon us this conscience? Over and over again we dare to directly disobey God's commands. It is a terrible thing to fall into the hands of the Living God. But the Lord of Hosts is long-suffering, and to repentant Christians He is the Father of Mercies. Yet it behooves us, Christians, to zealously watch every step we take, to be sure that we are walking in the path, that our Holy Church not only pointed out, but, as it were, even cut out for us by the stream of martyr's blood, by the wisdom of the Holy Spirit abiding in the sainted bishops of the universal councils, the night labor of praying and fasting fathers, and a host of pure, self-sacrificing, obedient women, such as Mary, Thekla, Barbara, Makrina. The Church says that in time of Lent we must fast, and we should not disobey, because our Holy Church is the Church of God, and she tells us what God Himself wills that we should do. If we have all the learning of the nineteenth century, it will appear as a blank before the simple words of the Church, spoken in the power of the Spirit of God. We cannot, and we have no right (for who gave us such a privilege), to excuse ourselves. We are with good intention, in simplicity of heart to obey the commandments of the Church, and not worry about adapting ourselves to the ways of the Church, for when we obey with our whole heart, with a strong desire to fulfill the holy commandments, then our Holy Mother Church adapts herself to the weakness of her faithful children. But let us turn back to the lesson pointed out for us. We may every day learn a new lesson about the next life, which is of so much importance, that the examples in this life are inexhaustible. Look around and observe. In this instance look into the kingdom of animals and birds. See the clean dove hovering over places that are clean, over the grain field, gathering seed for its young. Now look at the unsatiated raven, flapping its heavy wings around the meat market. And so we must strive to love a temperate life, that we may be beloved by angels, and hate all unnecessary luxury, so as not to fall with it into communion with demons.

Let us return with our memory to the commencement of our race, and experience will testify to that which we sometimes make light of. The law of fasting would not be given to us, had not the law of the first abstinence been transgressed. The stomach would not be named as an evil-minded thing, had not the pretext for pleasure entailed after it such consequences of sin. There would be no need of the plow and the laboring oxen, the planting of seed, the watering shower, the mutual change of the seasons of the year, the winter binding in fetters and the summer opening up all things. In a word, there would be no need of such periodically repeating toil, had not we, through the mistaken pleasure of our first parents, condemned ourselves to this round of labor. Yet, we were on the way of leading another kind of life, in comparison with what we see now, and which we hope to regain once more, when we are liberated from this life of passion by the resurrection. Such is the mercy of God's condescension towards us, that we should be again restored to the former dignity, which we had enjoyed through His love to man, and which mercy we did not carefully keep. Fast is a type of the future life, an imitation of the incorruptible existence. There are no feastings and sensual gratifications over there.

Do not flee from the difficulty of fast, but set up hope against the trial, and you will obtain the desired abstinence from food. Repeat to yourself the words of the pious: "Fast is bitter, but paradise is sweet; thirst is tormenting, but the spring, from which he who drinks will thirst never again, is at hand." The body is importunate, but the immaterial soul is much stronger — strength is dead, but nigh is the resurrection. Let us say to our much craving stomach what the Lord said to the tempter: *Man shall not live by bread alone, bid by every word of God.* Fast is not hunger, but a little abstinence from food, not an inevitable punishment, but a voluntary continence, not a servile necessity, but a free selection of the wise. Pray and you will be strengthened; call, and a prompt helper will come to your assistance.

Sermon on the Gospel
of the Prodigal

(First read: Luke 15:11–32)

You have heard today's Gospel. The parable of the "prodigal son" is not a thing new to you. You have heard of, you have seen the prodigal sin, and fall low, down, deep into all the consequential miseries of iniquity. If you do not know, you have heard of the boundless mercy of a pitying God. You may understand how a good father takes back to his heart his beloved child, once lost, but found again. You know the parable of the prodigal son. Then why is it that the Church, year after year, recalls to our memory this parable? She does so in order to strengthen us in the way of salvation. Until we have passed the final limit, and receive our sentence at the hands of the Divine Judge, we belong to the Church Militant, i.e. while we are on earth, we are obliged to continually struggle for the good.

In order to obtain conscientious peace, love, spiritual prosperity, and holiness, we must always battle with the evil. The more high and purely spiritual the condition is, which we strive to attain, the more fierce is the fight, and our warfare must be constant with wrong, infidelity, superstition, prejudice, and corruption. Indeed, we must overcome ourselves, we must get the better of self.

You, no doubt, have seen men and women wasting their living in the most hideous visible form of sin, but dare you stand in the awful presence of the Most Pure Being and Creator, and say that you are not a prodigal? Do you not wish to come back to God — the Heavenly Father? Sinners, yes, we are sinners! One of the greatest meditators on the ways of Divine Providence — the Prophet-King

David — in his confession to God, says: "*Thy commandment is very broad.*" And, in this light, there is not a commandment, or a law, which we have not transgressed.

Surely my time was not spent with harlots, some might say, but did you make careful use of your time, which is not yours, for it belongs to Him who gave it, and did you without wasting, treasure it so that it now bears a hundred fold of profit, pleasing to the Receiver of virtue in abundance? I had never lost control of myself, so that, by unawares, my table prove to be a scanty board of husks, and my companions a herd of swine. Yet, you may not assert that you beautified your soul with a holy character, nor did you enrich your intellect with an everlasting wisdom; and your heart, is it clean, does it expand so that the Holy Spirit freely makes His abode there? Does it know the needy and the deserving? Does it go out toward its neighbor, yearning to share with its very existence — giving up all self-interest, and even the comforts of an earthly life?

We, all of us, make up one household. We are members of one and the same family. And you will never taste of true happiness, nor know what it is to be blessed, until you have learned this lesson. You may be a younger son or daughter, but if you be the prodigal, remember, that in your *Father's House there is bread enough, and to spare; come to yourself*; consider your life, remember the free and confiding innocence of your first youth, now that you are firmly fastened, and yet lost, look within and find yourself. And when you have found yourself, you will easily find God. He will see you, while you are *coming, yet far off, your Father, and He will be moved with compassion, He will fold you in His arms and kiss you.*

If you are not a younger member of the family, may you not be the elder son of the Father? You may not be a lavish spendthrift, nor a wanderer, and you may enjoy the quiet of home, but are you secure? *The enemy may sow tares in the field of your heart, while you are comfortably asleep.* You may live in your father's house faithfully and continually, you may have the oversee of all the work, and the servants, yet are you secure? No, if you do not give yourself concern of the whereabouts of your younger brother, you are not secure for all time. You may be the oldest, you may know all the secrets of the household, the keys of all chests and doors may be in your possession, you may live in the Grace of God, and enjoy the light of your Heavenly Father's countenance, still, remember the elder son in the parable! For the want of charity for an erring one, a sinner, an inexperienced one, for one who labored under a wrong opinion, he — the heir and first-born — came in danger of losing all at the end. He was the cause of much anxiety to his father *who came out and entreated him.* This one's pride (a false pride it was) that suffered. The father had to reason with his son, who thought his sense of justice was being injured. In the absence of virtue, and charity — the principal one — we see the elder son blind to his own condition, for he dared to assert his rights, while justice belonged to the real owner, his loving Father.

And now, my brethren, if we be the elder members of God's family, let us think of the responsibility, and not fall from Grace, but continue in His House. To the young, and to the prodigal, if their conscience be not yet lost, the Divine voice calls, come to your Father, and tell Him all, He waits with open heart. Amen.

Sermon Preached on Orthodox Sunday

Who is so great a God as our God? Thou art the God that alone doest wonders.

On this first Sunday in Lent, the Church, in memory and in thanksgiving for her victory in the struggles and labors in protecting the true Faith against the contentions of evil-minded heretics, celebrates the "Triumph of Orthodox Christianity," and for this reason we call this day "Orthodox Sunday."

It was in 787 AD that the Church, in Universal Council assembled, decreed, among other resolutions and canonical acts, that it was lawful for Christians to use in their private and public worship sacred images, i.e., pictures of our Lord Jesus Christ, His Holy Mother, of the Saints, and sacred events in Biblical and Christian history, but, of course, when divine adoration was ascribed to God alone, and when reverence is offered in honor of His works — the objects which these cherished pictures represent to us.

The Christian doctrine necessary for our salvation, as revealed in Sacred Scripture and Tradition, has been expounded and delivered for us, free from all mixture of human and heretical interpretation, by the Seven Great Councils. The one mentioned before was the last, namely, the Seventh Ecumenical Council. These councils defined the teaching concerning the Persons of the Most Holy Trinity in the one Godhead, the advent in the world of the Son of God, the relations between ourselves and our Savior, the relations between the Church Militant on earth and the Church Triumphant in heaven, the Providence of God in our reward and in our punishment, the Apostolic Succession and Hierarchical Economy as necessary for the continuance of Christ's work in the world, the seven Sacraments, etc.

It was not long, however, when again heresy began to show itself in some of the branches of the Church, and when some ambitious people would impose upon the Church their personal and fallible opinions. To ward off the false shoots and upstarts, and to remind the Christians of the binding rules and canons of the Seven General Councils, a large assembly of Holy Fathers and teachers gathered in Constantinople in 842 AD, under the protection of the good Empress Theodora, and, mindful of the Divine Judgment pronounced of the Holy Spirit though it was by the condescendingly lovable Apostle St. Paul that *if any man love not the Lord Jesus Christ let him be Anathema Maranatha*, they declared: "To those who reject the councils of the Holy Fathers and their traditions which are agreeable to Divine Revelation, and which the Orthodox Catholic Church piously maintains, anathema!"

This council sat in convention during the first week of Great Lent. While fasting and praying, they collected all the decisions of the Seven General Councils. When Sunday came, they marched in solemn procession, bearing the holy cross, sacred images of our Lord, the Blessed Virgin and the Saints, being followed by a multitude of Christians devoutly chanting under the leadership of the learned monk well known by the name of St. Theodore the Studite, his newly composed hymn which you have heard today and which translated reads thus: "To Thy most pure Icon (image) we bow down, O Blessed One, praying for forgiveness of our sins, Christ our God; for, of Thine own will, Thou didst condescend to ascend the cross in flesh, and thereby to deliver Thy creatures from the yoke of the enemy. Therefore, we thankfully cry unto Thee, Thou hast filled all things with joy, O our Savior, Thou who earnest to save the world."

Having come into the Cathedral of St. Sophia, this religious and noted assemblage offered the most impressive praise service, or "Te Deum," ever known in the grand liturgies of the Holy Orthodox Church. We have in the words of the Psalmist David the key-note which re-echoed in the thunder of anathemas and resounded in the peals of praise of this complete and universal thanksgiving service: *Who is so great a God as our God? Thou art the God that alone doest wonders!* Here were recounted all the false teachings condemned by the Ecumenical Councils, and even persons were anathematized for willfully adhering to heresy, who did not repent of their sins, and earnestly seek the truth by their return to membership in the Church of Christ. Among such were those "who deny the existence of God, and unreasonably maintain that the world existeth of itself, and that all things happen through fate and without the providence of God; those who insolently dare to say that the All-pure Virgin Mary, before her bringing forth, in her bringing forth, and after her bringing forth, was not a virgin; those who believe not that the Holy Spirit gave wisdom to the Prophets and Apostles, and through them proclaimed to us the true way to everlasting salvation, and that He confirmed them by wonders, nor believe that now He dwelleth in the hearts of the faithful and true Christians, leading them into all truth; those who deny the immortality of the soul, who reject the councils of the Holy Fathers, and the traditions unanimous with the divine revelation which the Orthodox Catholic Church with veneration preserveth; those who defame and blaspheme the holy icons which the Holy Church useth to remember the works of God and of His Saints, so that they who look upon the same may be incited to fear God and to imitate what they see; and those who say the icons are idols."

It may be necessary before we proceed to explain the word anathema; it means condemnation and excommunication until restored after sincere repentance. In some cases, it may not be only a temporal ban, but a curse. Indeed, there are some members of the Church today, Christians, who do not fully realize that the Church of Christ is a living organism, which, through the supernatural indwelling of the Holy Spirit, exists as a moral being, empowered within her sphere not only to bless, but also to curse. Such ones of course do not read the Bible. Those who studied the Epistles of the Apostles know that it was required of the Corinthians to *put away from among themselves that wicked person* (1 Cor. 5:13). Likewise the command was given to Titus, hear: *A man that is an heretic after the first and second admonition reject* (Tit. 3:10). Did not our Lord Jesus Christ say: *If thy brother neglect to hear the Church, let him be to thee as an heathen man and a publican?* (Matt. 18:17.) And again our Lord speaks: *Whatsoever ye shall bind on earth shall be bound in heaven; and whatsoever ye shall loose on earth shall be loosed in heaven* (Matt. 18:18).

Since the time of this council which we have just now been considering, the Church, annually, until our day "has celebrated the triumph of Truth over heresy, and blessed the memory of, as well as commended the work of all them that by words, writings, teachings, and sufferings, as also by a life well-pleasing to God, have contended for Orthodoxy as her defenders and helpers." Among those now living are named: The Royal and Imperial Benefactors, the Orthodox Patriarchs of Constantinople, Alexandria, Antioch, and Jerusalem, the Holy Synods of the Russian and other Orthodox Churches, the Most Reverend Bishops, the Reverend Clergy, all right-believing Christians who, through saving faith and good works, are expecting everlasting blessedness. Thus the Church today in most of the diocesan cathedrals throughout the world, while joyfully praising and honoring them that *submitted their understanding to the obedience of the Divine Revelation,* and have contended for the same by following the Holy Scriptures and holding fast the traditions of the primitive Church, at the same time "humbly supplicates Almighty God for those who, by heresy or by schism, have set themselves against His evangelical truth that He may soften their hearts, open their ears that they may recognize His voice, heal their corruptions and deliver them out of error."

When we see how the Lord of creation and the Shepherd of His elect flock has preserved His Church undefiled and whole through long ages of the most terrible temptations, and when we hear the prophet cry out that *God wills no one to be lost, but that all may come to repentance and to the tinder standing of truth, we cannot else but cry out: Who is so great a God as our God? Thou art the God that alone doest wonders.*

Sermon Preached on the Third Sunday of Great Lent

Whosoever will come after Me, let him deny himself, and take up his cross and follow Me.
(Mark 8:34)

This third Sunday of Great Lent is the first day of the Holy Cross week. In the midst of this holy season the Church allows her children to taste of the sweetness of the tree. In the course of his forty days' journey over the solitary wilderness of penance, the weary wayfarer comes to a tree, its shade inviting, its fruit beneficial. He throws off his burden; with composure and confidence, he nestles at the foot of the wood, and is refreshed. And this is just what the Church of God prepares for the sincere followers of Jesus Christ. Were we capable of understanding the Almighty's plan, carried out by the Church for our salvation, what consolation and benefit, both spiritual and temporal, would be ours.

Whosoever will come after Me, let him deny himself, and take up his cross and follow Me. This is what Jesus said to the multitude that followed Him. They followed Him, some from curiosity, anxious to see a miracle performed, others in earnest, eager to listen to the words that came from the lips of Him, *who taught as one having the power*, while there were those which followed in humble obedience, grateful for the charity bestowed on them, or on their loved ones, by the *Prophet of Nazareth*, and, alas! there were some that dogged every step of this *Good Shepherd*, who led his human flock over the green hills of Galilee, or quenched their thirst with *living water* down in the *valley of Jordan*, spies — which were to take Him and put Him to a horrible death — nailing Him hands and feet to a crossed wood. As he turned toward the people, He addressed them, saying: *For what shall it profit a man if he shall gain the whole world and lose his own soul. Whosoever shall be ashamed of Me and of My words in this adulterous and sinful generation, of him also shall the Son of Man be ashamed when He cometh in the glory of His Father with the holy angels* (Mark 8:36, 38).

Jesus has nowadays many followers desirous of consolation, but few of tribulation. All desire to rejoice with Him, few are willing to endure anything for Him. Many reverence His miracles, few follow the ignominy of His cross.

What cross is it which our Lord would have us bear? Hardships, sickness, slander, persecutions, poverty, desertion of friends, the heavy cares of public responsibility, yea — and death itself. We may for a time be forsaken of God; sometimes we are troubled by our neighbors, yea — and by those whom we love dearly; and what is more, often-times we may even become weary of ourselves. If Christ bore the cross for all mankind, Christians are expected to help carry the cross of at least some of their neighbors. But how? By bearing in patience the failings and weakness of our neighbor. By not becoming ill-tempered when a brother or sister sets forth his or her opinion as to this or that. By hushing the serpent's hiss of envy, and showing sympathy and gladness when one either above or beneath us proves himself worthy of public praise, though we ourselves may not be so much as noticed. By denying ourselves the wicked pleasure of making jest of a soul which goes about acting strangely, and especially when we do not understand nor see plainly the results of such conduct. By denying ourselves the luxuries which may supply the want of many who suffer misery.

Whosoever will come after Me, let him deny himself, and take up his cross and follow Me (Mark 8:34). O how powerful is the pure love of Jesus, which is mixed with no self-interest, with no self-love! Are not those to be called mercenary who are ever seeking consolations? The Holy Fathers of the Church tell us that "such are lovers of themselves, but not of Christ. Where shall one be found, the Holy Fathers continue, who is willing to serve God for naught?" In their great fervor to serve, in their deep and vast love for God, the Holy Fathers had not noticed how they themselves were growing into perfection by following our Lord Jesus Christ. Yes, in their persons and lives we have many types and good examples unto the salvation of our souls; yea, and unto the salvation of the world. And so we must lose all that which unites us to this world that is passing away. If we link our life with and make it one with that of the common animal, subject our reason to vain pursuits and the better qualities of our spirit to passions of the flesh, then we lose our life, *for dust will go to dust. But whosoever shall lose his life for the sake of Christ and the Gospel, the same shall save it*; i.e., he who is dead to self, when one becomes separated from the principles which make one long for the pleasure and desire of this world's life, in which there is no thought for eternity, *the same shall save his life*, though he seemingly perish in discomfort and suffer banishment at the hands of a self-idolizing society, for he lives through Christ and the Gospel with the spiritual life which never grows old and is everlasting.

During the whole of this week, the Church is continually reminding us of the cross. And many a weary soul is sighing for rest... Shall my burden be lessened? There seems to be for some no end to sickness. The cares of duty are constant and heavy. There are those which cannot find a friend who could understand their inmost soul and soothe their troubled conscience. Oh! that God would give me that inward peace, they cry without faith and in despair. Deny yourself all passions which are prompted by selfish motives and by interests, which will pass away as the light of day is lost in the darkness of night; deny these passions all gratification whatever. What a hard lot! you might say. The circumstances surrounding our lives are very pressing... What will people say? We must keep up with the rest of the world. We are in a pitiable condition. No one should criticize us. We should be left to do as we please. But the Church says we must give up the pleasure of being even a little ambitious. Yes, the Church of Christ says: Forsake all false ambition. Christians, be not discouraged. The Infinite Wisdom itself watches over your salvation. In selfishly moping over our own woes, over our little cross, have we forgotten the Cross of Christ? The Church, then, will remind us of it.

This week is set aside for the worship of the cross. Here is the *tree of life*. The cross that our Lord Jesus Christ carried to Mount Calvary and made it an altar, on which He offered Himself up to God the Father as a sacrifice. Let us come to the shade of this tree and rest. This wood has been planted for our own benefit. Let us in holy meditation bring to our mind the suffering of that bleeding form outstretched above us, although it is difficult and for some impossible to feel for one moment the anguish of that cross, borne all the weary way from Bethlehem; then our little crosses, which we have merited by our sins, will not be a yoke of thorns, but an altar on which we may offer up to God our love. Our course is not finished. The road lies before … Lent is still in season. Now, while we enjoy the protection of the cross, let us also supply ourselves with strength, i.e., the Grace of God, for the journey is not finished and the way is so uncertain. Let us refresh and strengthen ourselves with a supply of the fruit of the wood. The fruit is the flesh and blood of our Savior, who was sacrificed in order to appease the righteous wrath of the Infinite God for the sins of all mankind, beginning with the disobedience of Adam. Shall not our Creator receive us when we humbly and gratefully come to Him together with His infinitely beloved, His Only-begotten, *as the Light which is of Light*, His Son Jesus Christ?

Christians, ye who come to this tree, go not away without tasting of its sweet fruit. Our Holy Church brings us this week to the cross to be refreshed by renewing our spirit, so that our own cross be not a burden but a blessing. Do we forget our duty towards our Mother Church? Yes, unfortunately some do. May we not let go unheeded the advice of the parent, which has given us birth in baptism for a new life, but come to the foot of the cross and cast off our yoke of sins, be absolved of all that which is impure and wicked, either in thought, or in desire, or in deed, by confession, and in holy communion with Jesus Christ be reconciled to God. Amen.

Sermon for the Fourth Sunday in Great Lent

For He (Jesus) taught His disciples, and said unto them: the Son of Man is delivered up into the hands of men, and they shall kill Him; and when He is killed, after three days He shall rise again (Mark 9:31).

Christ the Savior, having spoken the sorrowful word that *they shall kill Him,* adds the joyful ones that *He on the third day shall rise again,* concluding thus that we may know that after sorrows there always follows happiness. If there were no temptations there would be no crown, no hardships, no rewards; were there no conflicts, nor would there be any honors, no sorrows, no comforts; if there were no winter there would be no summer.

And this we may observe not only in people, yet also in the seeds which are thrown into the earth; and here a heavy rain and much cold are necessary, so that a stem spring up green, bearing its ear of plenty. Let us sow also in the time when spiritual misfortune visits us that we may reap in the summer; let us sow tears that we may reap happiness. According to the Prophet of God: *They that sow in tears shall reap in joy* (Ps. 123:5). Not so beneficial is the rain which pours over the seeds as the rain of tears, which gives the power of growth and ripens the seed of piety. As the tiller of the soil cuts deep into the earth with his plow, preparing a safe place for the seed that they may hide in the very bowels of the earth and safely take root, thus also should we with misfortune and sadness, as with a plow, touch the depths of our heart.

The holy Prophet would convince us thus, saying: *Tear open your hearts but not your garments.* Let us tear open our hearts so that, if there be any evil plant or evil thought within us, we may pluck it out with the root and cleanse the field for seeds of holy devotion. If we do not renew the field now, if we do not sow now, if we do not shed tears now, when it is Lent — in this time of sorrow and fast — at what other time, then shall we be afflicted? Can it be in the time of ease and pleasure? No, it cannot be then, for ease and pleasure lead to carelessness, while sorrow compels the soul, which is beset with many attractions on all sides, to look within itself.

The farmer having sown the seeds, which he gathered with much labor, prays for rain; and one, not knowing the work, with amazement looks upon all, and, perhaps, thinks so within himself: "What is that man doing? He throws away that which he gathered; but not that only, he yet carefully mixes it with the earth; and that is not all, for he prays that what he has sown may decay." Quite contrarily does the farmer when he sees the coming clouds overshadow the sky he rejoices, for he does not look at the present, but to the future; he does not think of the thunder, but of the sheaves; not of the decaying seeds, but of the yellow ripe stalks. Thus should we look, not at the sorrow of the present, but at the benefit which is derived from it. If we be on our guard, we will not only suffer no evil from sorrow, but derive much consolation; but if we be careless, the very enjoyment of quiet will turn to be hurtful for us. To the careless, one thing and another is evil, but to the diligent one thing and another is profitable. As gold retains its brightness when it lies in the water, and becomes still brighter when it is cast into the furnace, so we see the very opposite when if clay and straw are put into water; the one dissolves, the other rots. Now this is just the case with the righteous and the sinner; the first living in quiet remains bright like the gold which was put into the water, and being afflicted with temptation becomes brighter still, as the gold which passed through the fires of the refinery. But the sinner, although enjoying ease, dissolves and decays, as the straw and clay thrown into water or the furnace, where it burns and perishes.

Let us not be sad for present misfortune. If you have any sins, they will be easily uprooted by sorrow. And if you are the possessor of a virtue, it will become brighter for having undergone temptation. If you will continually watch, you will be beyond the reach of harm, as the cause of falling generally is not the kind of a temptation, but the carelessness of those tempted. And so, if you would enjoy quiet, do not seek pleasure, but strive to make your soul capable of being patient, because if this quality is wanting in you, you will not only be conquered by temptation, but sooner fall a prey to the spirit of desolation which ease will bring upon you. As the storms of wind do not uproot a strong wood with its roots, but on the contrary from constant blowing on from all sides it becomes firmer, so does the holy soul, although overwhelmed with afflictions, it bends not, but becomes invigorated with a higher energy. How might we, a generation of the New Covenant, become justified and forgiven when we with difficulty overcome human temptations, while Job, the much afflicted, outbore with such alacrity a most sore temptation in the days before Grace, of the Old Dispensation?

Are you sad, beloved, because the Most Good Provider through sorrowing brought you to the thought of eternal salvation? God can put an end today to all troubles; but He will not destroy sorrow until He sees a change in us, until repentance really and strongly works within us. The goldsmith will not take the metal from the fire before it is purified, and God will not withdraw the tempest clouds before we are perfected by corrections. He who sends the affliction knows when the time comes to hold its stay. A player of the cithern does not tighten too much the strings, else they snap, nor does he freely loosen them, else the harmony of sound be lost. So does the Lord with our souls, which He will not leave in continual ease, nor in everlasting sorrow, ordering the one and the other according to His wisdom. The Almighty does not allow us to enjoy quiet without a change that we may not become more careless; nor does He keep us ever in sorrow that we may not fall in despair. Since we are occupied with this question, let us decide to wait for our Heavenly Father's own time for putting an end to troubles, while we ourselves will pray and lead a life of devotion: because to turn to righteousness and live in the faith belongs to our obligation, but to quiet our sorrow is the work of God. God who is mightier than you, who are afflicted in temptation, desires to quench that fire, but He waits for your salvation. Therefore, as sorrow is begotten from ease, likewise we should wait for sorrow to give us quiet. It is not always winter, nor always summer; the tempest does not always blow, nor does the quiet always last; it is not always night, nor all one day. Thus also with us when we are sad, a change comes, we feel lighter, our hope is stronger — if we pray and in time of sorrow continually thank God.

And so let us enclose ourselves on all sides with truly good and charitable works, and thereby be saved from the anger of God. Let us make the members of our body the organs of righteousness; let us teach the whole body to serve only the cause of virtue. Then we will be delivered from present dangers, appease the Most High, and reach that inexpressible bliss, of which may we all be made worthy by the Grace and love for us of our Lord Jesus Christ, through Whom be glory to the Father with the Holy Spirit, now, ever and forever. Amen.

Thoughts for Good Friday at the Passions and Burial of Christ

It was our earnest desire to pursue the story of our Savior's trials and His crucifixion; but when I *looked on Him whom they pierced*, my spirit failed before the terrible sight; *I could not watch with Him another hour*, and yet I could not leave the hallowed scene. It seemed as though I saw Him brought back from Herod where the soldiers mocked Him. I followed Him through the streets again as the cruel priests pushed through the wild crowd and hastened Him back to Pilate's court. My ears sounded with the cry: *Crucify Him, crucify Him! Give us Barabbas, the robber; let Barabbas go; but Christ, the King of the Jews. Jesus, the Savior, He must die!* And there He stood, *who loved me* and gave Himself for me, *like a lamb in the midst of wolves*, with none to pity and none to help Him.

As Jesus Christ hung apparently helpless upon the cross, He had only to utter the word, and in a moment more than twelve legions of angels (what an invincible force of energetic beings!) would be ready to succor and defend. But to have shunned all pain and anguish, to have refused the cup which His Father had given Him, to have rejected the cross — this would have been to leave man to his doom; this He could not do. And so, *He saved others, Himself He could not save.*

Our Lord for a long time bore His cross, as though He felt not its weight; even from the time of the most helpless age of humanity, when He was born in the smallest town of the smallest kingdom on the earth, when there was no home, no cradle for Him, and when, except His humble mother with her guardian, none but a few shepherds took any interest in His birth; He bore His cross till at length He was completely delivered up on it. We could not follow Jesus throughout in His earthly life. During these holy days, we have but endeavored to follow Him only through a few of the last scenes of His entire sacrifice. In a measure we understand, and we feel in His sufferings, as His body, in its weight drooped, being sustained but by four nails, as the cross was raised over the multitude of people on the hill and then the shock as it went down into its socket. Only a chosen few, and likewise in a small measure can they understand how He — who prayed, *Father forgive them, for they know not what they do* — has stretched out his arms on the wood in order to embrace a sinful world. But no mortal knoweth how *the Word was with God, and the Word was God.* The Word of God is not bound by death. As a word from the lips dies not entirely away at the moment its sound ceases, but rather gathers new strength, and passing through the senses penetrates the minds and hearts of the hearers, so also the Hypostatical Word of God, the Son of God, in His saving incarnation, whilst dying in the flesh, *fills all things* with His spirit and might. Thus when Christ waxeth faint and becometh silent on the cross, then is it that heaven and earth raise their voice unto Him, and the dead preach the resurrection of the crucified, and the very stones cry out. *And the sun was darkened, and the veil of the temple was rent in the midst; and the earth did quake and the rocks rent; and the graves were opened, and many bodies of the saints which slept arose.*

O sinful man, O nature, bereft of perfection. O reason, a mind earthly winged, down low, stoop thou under cover of repentant shame before the light of this grave. Christian, there is no other place for thee today but by the Cross of Christ. "Broken and distributed is the Lamb of God, which is broken, yet not severed, which is ever eaten, yet never consumed, but sanctifying those that participate." Therefore, come, ye sons of toil and ye daughters of Eve; come, come, ye citizens of the easy-going wide world; see, His side is now and forever opened for us. O mother, sufferest thou for thy children? Bring them to the tomb of Jesus and quiet thyself in the stillness of His silence. Brother, sister, behold in the Savior thy kinsman. And thou poor, lonely wan-derer, here He quietly lies in one place that thou mayest find Jesus, thy only Friend. We come, who labor in Thy infinite sorrow for the sins of mankind, we who are heavy laden with our infirmities, we come and supplicate before Thy breathless form.

Uniting all things in one, grant that we all may inseparably be one with Thee and Thy Father, O Lord Jesus Christ! Thou that reconcil-est all, grant that all may be of one mind in faith and in love toward Thee. Thou that bears not with the envious and contentious, destroy all wicked heresy and separations. O Jesus! Thou that lovest and piti-est, gather into one flock all wandering sheep. Thou that givest peace to all, still the voice of spite and dispute among those who call upon Thy name. Thou who communicatest to us the very Body and very Blood of Thyself, grant that we truly be flesh of Thy flesh and bone of Thy bones. O Jesus, the God of our hearts, unite us with Thee, now and forever. Amen.

Sermon on the Gospel
Relating to the Impotent

John 5:15

Jesus went up to Jerusalem. These are the words which begin the Gospel appointed to be read at the Liturgy on this Sunday. How many thousands must have hurried to those *feasts* in honor of the *One true God*, in that splendid city of types and symbols of things not yet made clear, and to be manifested in the midst of pagan and barbarous nations! It must have been a great multitude that almost continually *went up to Jerusalem*. So did our Lord Jesus Christ go with them. He was in the crowd, sometimes known, but most often *His own received Him not*. Those who *went up to Jerusalem* in those days went to the only one Temple, where the only divinely authorized priesthood had offered the one acceptable type of the all-available sacrifice. To be understood, in plainer language, we may say of them that they went to church. There is nothing extraordinary; the going is a simple fact of going to church. But how did they go? Absurd? Does it seem to you so? Certainly, it seems that most people go along in the same way. At the bottom of the movement which makes people go somewhere, there is an intention, and I think that when people go to church they go with a fixed purpose. If you ask how they go, with the purpose of disclosing their one or several intentions, then I answer with the word of God as recorded by St. Paul: *For who among men knoweth the things of a man, save the spirit of the man, which is in him? Even so the things of God none knoweth, save the Spirit of God.* But for our edification and salvation on this as well as on several other memorable occasions, we are permitted to see and to learn how our Lord Jesus Christ *went up to Jerusalem,* and consequently how He went to Church.

He went to Jerusalem *at the feasts* in order to give a larger number of people an opportunity of seeing and hearing the Truth. He went to *the house of His Father,* and openly manifested His power as the Son of God. Before the doctors and lawyers He testified to the Old Testament prophecies as the *Messiah.* He passed by the way of sufferers so that He might help them, and where He was not expected, there He was found. He gave courage to those who had lost hope, and those who hoped on and long He rewarded with His grace. Where an angel by stirring the water cured a sick one in a year, He, the Lord of Angels, heals both body and soul, be it of one, or a hundred, or a thousand, and now as He did then and ever will as long as one be found who will surrender himself as others have done: *Lord, Thou canst make me whole!*

But let us return to Bethesda, not because it is the public hospital where lay a multitude of the needy, but because, as impotent folk ourselves, we will find there on this occasion the bread of life and the very source of the never-ending stream of living water. Let us follow Christ through *the five porches, where a certain man was which had been thirty and eight years in his infirmity. When Jesus saw him lying, and knew that he had been now a long time in that case, He saith unto him: Wouldst thou be made whole? The sick man answered Him: Sir, I have no man, when the water is troubled, to put me into the pool; but while I am coming another steppeth down before me.*

Why is it that Jesus passed by all the others and stopped by this one? He did so in order to show His power and also His love for mankind: His power, because the disease had become incurable and the weakness of the sick one was beyond hope; His love for mankind, because the Provider and Merciful One, in preference to others, looked upon such who were especially worthy of pity and charity. Let us not quickly pass by this place without giving our attention to the thirty-eight years during which this sick one continued in his weakness. Let all who struggle with continual poverty, or pass their lifetime in sickness, or those who find themselves in difficult and threatening circumstances, or cast down in the storm and tempest of sudden troubles, let them all hear of it. No one can be so faint-hearted, so mean and unfortunate as not to bear all that happens to us manfully and with all cheerfulness, when looking upon this special one at the watering place of Bethesda. If he suffered for twenty years, or ten, or only five years, would they not be sufficient to break the strength of his soul? But he remains in that condition for thirty-eight years, and does not break down in spirit, but shows great patience. Hear his wisdom, for indeed a Christian may lend ear to this sick one's philosophizing. Jesus came up and said to him: *Wouldst thou be made whole?* Who does not know such a thing? Why of course the impotent desired to become well. Then for what reason does he ask? Certainly not because of ignorance: for Him who knows the secret thoughts of people, that which was apparent and open to all was to Him the more so simple. Why does He ask? As He said to the centurion: *I will come and heal him*, not because He did not know at first what his answer would be, but because foreseeing and knowing well the answer He wished to give the centurion the opportunity to disclose before all his piety, which was concealed as if under a shadow, and to say: *Lord, I am not worthy that Thou shouldst come under my roof*. So also this impotent, of the nature of whose answer He knew, the Lord asks does he wished to be healed, not because He knew that not Himself, but for the purpose of giving the sick one a chance to speak out of his misfortune and to become a teacher of patience. If the Savior had healed this man silently, we would have lost much by not learning of the strength of his soul.

Christ does not rule the present only, but He offers to the future also His condescending and great care. In the impotent He showed us a teacher of patience and courage for all times to come, having put him to the necessity of answering the question: *Wouldst thou be made whole?* But what of him? The impotent was not offended; he did not become angry; he said not to the inquirer: Thou seest me infirm, thou knowest that my sickness is of long standing, and thou inquirest, do I desire to regain my health? But did you come to laugh at my misfortunes and to make light of other people's troubles? You know how faint-hearted the sick become when they lay in bed even one year; but whose sickness lasts for thirty-eight years, does it not become natural for such a one to lose all better knowledge, wasting away in the course of so long a time? The impotent, however, said nothing like this, nor even thought of it, but he answered with much modesty: *Sir, I have no man, when the water is troubled, to put me into the pool.* See how many troubles unitedly grieved this man: his disease, his poverty, and the absence of a lifting, a helping hand. *While I am coming, another steppeth down before me.* This is that which is the saddest of all, and it ought to have softened even a stone. Does it not seem as if you can see this man each year creeping along until he has crept up to the very side of the pool, then stopping each year just before the reach of a bright hope? And it is the more burdensome, as he experienced this not for two, or three, or ten, but for thirty-eight years. He did everything in his power, but did not obtain the result; the labor was accomplished, but the reward for labor went to another one during all these many years; and, what is more burdensome, he saw others healed.

The good fortune of others around us compels us to see plainly in the contrast our own misfortune; it was the same then with the impotent. Nevertheless, for so long a time he struggled with sickness, with poverty, and with loneliness, seeing that others were healed, while he himself, although he always tried, but never could reach his desire, and not hoping in the future to liberate himself of suffering, with all this against him he did not retreat, but renewed his endeavor each year. And we, if we once pray to God and do not obtain what we have asked for, we immediately become disappointed and fall into extreme carelessness, so that we stop praying and lose fervor. May we according to worth praise the impotent, as we may in the same way condemn our negligence? What justification and forgiveness may we expect when he was patient for thirty-eight years, while we become despondent so soon. To this one it has been said: *Arise, take up thy bed and walk.* And if we be or be not infirm in body, or soul, mind, character, or condition, it is in every instance demanded of us all to take up our cross and to follow Him, our Lord Jesus Christ, with whom, after a faithful following, we shall see ourselves gloriously resurrected.

Because Jesus did these things on the Sabbath the Jews persecuted Him. When persecuted for doing the works which proclaimed Him to be the Redeemer of the world, did our Lord justify Himself before His enemies and prove the Divine right of His most exalted mission? If He did not, then how could we, even to this day, hope in our salvation? Let us see how Jesus, on this occasion, has justified Himself; for the manner in which He proves His innocence shows us whether He belongs to the number of such who are ruled, or to the free, to those who serve, or whether He is of those who command. His action seemed to be a great iniquity, a sin against the law; for he who once gathered wood on the Sabbath was according to the law stoned to death for carrying a burden on the Sabbath (Num. 15:32, 36). Now Christ was accused of the same crime, namely, that He did not keep the Sabbath. Does He ask forgiveness as a servant and as a man under subjection, or does He appear as one who has power and independence as a Master, who is above the law and who Himself giveth the commandments? How does He justify Himself? *My Father*, says He, *worketh even until now, and I work.* Do you see His might? If He was lower or lesser than the Father, then what He had said would not be counted in His acquittal, but it would be to a greater accusation and to a greater condemnation. If one does something which is lawful to be done only by one who is above Him, and then having been taken and given to judgment, he says: as another higher one has done so, I also have done so, he would not only free himself from the charge in this way, but he would subject himself to a greater accusation and sentence, because to take upon one's self that which is above one's dignity can be done only by a self-conceited and proud person. Therefore, if Christ were lower than the Father, then what He had said would not be to His justification, but to a greater condemnation. But as *He is equal with the Father*, there is no fault in the words of Jesus Christ.

To understand the better what has been said, let us remember that His disciples had once broken the Sabbath in the field by pulling ears of corn and eating them; now He violated it Himself; the Jews accused them, and now they accuse Him. We will now investigate as to how He clears them and how He justifies Himself, so that we may learn from the difference between one and the other of the superiority of His justification. How did He justify His disciples? *Have you not read what David did when he hungered?* (Matt. 12:3). Defending creature-servants, He calls to mind David, a fellow-servant like unto themselves, but justifying Himself He reaches out with His speech to the Father: *My Father worketh, and I work.* Perhaps someone might ask: What kind of work does Jesus speak of, if *after six days God rested from all His works?* (Gen. 2:2). It is the everyday, the continual guidance and providence, for God not only made all nature, but He also keeps His creation. Do you refer to the angels, the archangels, or to the higher powers, and, in a word, to all things visible and invisible? Yes, all are under His providence, and if it would go outside the realm of His activity, then it falls to pieces, becomes destroyed and would perish. And so our Lord, desiring to show that He is the provider and not the object of providence, the worker and not the object of activity, He has therefore said: *My Father worketh, and I work,* thereby proving His equality with the Father, and to whom with the Holy Spirit be all glory now and to ages of ages. Amen.

Sermon for the Sunday When the Gospel of the Blind Is Read

(Read first the ninth chapter of St. John)

Τhis is the Gospel for today. What lesson have we to learn on this day? We must find the substance in these words, and feed on it, for it is spiritual food. When we have digested this Divine food, it will be assimilated with our natures, and our humanity will become purer, brighter, stronger, yea — and perpetual, so long as it lives with the Word of God, for hath not the Savior Himself said when the devil tempted Him who hungered in the wilderness: *That man shall not live by bread alone, but by every word that proceedeth out of the mouth of God?* So then, have we considered the Gospel while being read? If so, we find that the principal subject of it is the miracle which was worked by our Lord Jesus Christ. Next, we observe the man who was the object of the miracle, and finally we get a perspective of the condition. The circumstances which surrounded this miracle were most unfavorable for the blind man's confirmation in the faith, although he succeeded against such materialistic odds, and likewise for an open manifestation of the glory of the Wonder-worker Himself, yet the greatness of which became the more conspicuous as passion-bound opinions, systems and classes strived to overcome or, in the least, to belittle it.

When I stop to meditate, it seems that I am transported to the green hills of Judea, where the common folk of both hill country and populous valley are all astir with lively discussions in the midst of their every-day duties, as in their homes they go about to and fro, and, mind you, it is all about religion and politics; religion first and

politics after — insomuch as it is related with the proud nature of a
people, who boasted of being the chosen race of God, who expected
His messenger, and were to be ruled by none other than the Messiah Himself, unto all ages. It was a day of expectations, indeed. The
intellect of the masses had been sharpened to a turning point. The
very "times" themselves were full with signs. Everybody was inquir-
ing. The people willingly divided themselves into two sets: those that
taught and those that were taught. The nearer that some of them had
gotten to the truth, the more danger there was of taking falsehood
for the truth, and thereby more danger of *two blind men falling into
one pit*. Passions, although with a semblance of a higher quality, yet
human and materialistic, ruled the hour. In such a midst Christ, the
only true teacher of men, had come. No one condemned false doctrine so energetically as this teacher had done, and no one had taught
with such invincible strength and power as He did. Now the whole
company of teachers arose against this One, and, notwithstanding
their divisions, they knew how to agree in one and the same decision
which suited them all, and that was: That *He led the multitude astray*
(John 7:12), *He speaketh blasphemies* (Luke 5:21), *He perverteth our
nation* (Luke 23:2), and, at the end, for His teaching said they: *He is
worthy of death* (Matt. 26:66). But they could not destroy the work
of Him, whom they hated, for the people did see in Him *The Great
Prophet* (Luke 7:16). Above His calling as a teacher, He had the merits
of a miracle worker. What now could His angry enemies do or say
against this?

Now they would do as they have done at that time, viz: murdered
Him. But His works remain, and for that the glory of His resurrection
is the brighter. When the different conditions of a changing world, together with the many representatives of opinions have exhausted their
machinery, all their means, and wasted their fine scholastical dialec-
tics, while the simple facts, told by him who had once been blind, remain as simple facts, which he — who now sees — will not renounce,
then society answers and says to the followers of Jesus Christ: "You
were altogether born in sins, and do you teach us?" When Christians

cannot be subdued, nor compelled to follow the ways of politicians or the world in general, then they are left all to themselves. *And they cast Him out.*

The Son of God, manifesting His power in miracles that we may desire Him alone and thereby become strong in faith — this is the lesson that we are to learn today. Now the learned tell us that the nineteenth century (which happily is in its death-throes) requires "advanced thought." I wish the nineteenth century was over; we have heard it bragged about so much that one actually gets sick with the nineteenth century. We are told that this is too sensible a century to need or accept the same Gospel as the first, second and third centuries. Yet these were the centuries of martyrs and confessors, the centuries of heroes, the centuries that conquered all the gods of Greece and Rome, the centuries of holy glory, and all this because they were the centuries of the Gospel. But now we are so enlightened that our ears, strange to say, really ache for something fresh, and under the influence of so-called refined literature (how about ordinary novels?) our beliefs are dwindling down from mountains to ant-hills, and we ourselves from giants to pygmies.

By God's grace some of us abide by the Orthodox Faith, and mean to preach the same Gospel which the saints received at first. It is a foundation which we dare not change. It must be the same, world without end, for Jesus Christ is the same yesterday, today, and forever. Amen.

Sermon on the Feast of the Ascension[6]

And while they looked steadfastly toward heaven as He went up, behold, two men stood by them in white apparel, which also said: Ye men of Galilee, why stand ye gazing up into heaven? (Acts 1:10, 11).

The "two men in white apparel," who immediately after the ascension of the Lord appeared to the Apostles and asked them why they stood gazing up into heaven, were without doubt themselves inhabitants of heaven; therefore, it is not to be supposed that this was displeasing to them, or that they desired to direct the gaze of those men of Galilee elsewhere. No. They desire only to put an end to the inert amazement of the Apostles when saying: *Why stand ye gazing up into heaven?* Having aroused them from their amazement, they draw them into meditation, and teach them and us with what thoughts we should gaze into heaven, following our Lord Jesus who hath ascended thither. *This same Jesus*, they added, *which is taken up from you into heaven, shall come in like manner as you have seen Him go into heaven.*

The disciples of the Savior then beheld the exact fulfillment of His words which Mary Magdalene had recounted to them: *I ascend unto My Father and your Father, and to My God and your God.* They could not but conclude that those joyful visitations which He had bestowed upon them during the forty days after His resurrection from the dead, those instructive conversations with Him, that pal-

---

[6] This sermon was written and delivered by the author a few days after reading a most beautiful, but lengthy, sermon in the Russian language by the celebrated Metropolitan Philaret of Moscow.

pable communion between them and His divine humanity, were at that moment ended. When neither hand nor voice could any longer reach Him, they followed Him with their eyes, eager to detain Him; *they looked steadfastly toward heaven as He went up.* We can conceive what an immeasurable bereavement the Apostles must have felt after the ascension into heaven of Jesus, who as all and everything in the world to them; and it is this very bereavement for which the heavenly powers hasten to console them when telling them that *this same Jesus... shall come.*

In considering the circumstances of the ascension of Christ into heaven, we may first note the blessing which He then gave to the Apostles, *and it came to pass,* says the Evangelist Luke, *while He blessed them He was parted from them and carried up into heaven.* What an endless current of the grace of Christ is thus revealed unto us, Christians! The Lord begins a blessing, and before its completion ascends into heaven; *for while He blessed them He was carried up into heaven.* Thus even after His ascension does He still continue invisibly to impart His blessing. It flows and descends continuously upon the Apostles; through them it is diffused upon those whom they bless in the name of Jesus Christ; those who have received the blessing of Christ through the Apostles spread it among others; and thus do all who belong to the Holy Catholic and Apostolic Church become partakers of the one blessing of Christ. *As the dew of Herman that descended upon the mountain of Zion,* so does this blessing of peace descend upon every soul that riseth above passions and lusts, above vanity and the cares of the world; as an indelible seal does it stamp those who are of Christ in such a manner that at the end of the world He will by this very sign call them forth from the midst of all mankind, saying, *Come ye blessed!*

And now, my brethren, let us consider how needful it is for us to endeavor to gain now and to preserve this blessing of the Ascended Lord, which descends upon us also through the Apostolic Church. If we have received and preserved it, we shall, at the future advent of Jesus Christ, be called together with the Apostles and the saints to participate in His kingdom: *Come ye blessed!* But if, when He shall call *the blessed of His Father*, this blessing either be not found in us, or we be found in possession only of the false blessing of men who themselves have not inherited the blessing of the Heavenly Father by grace and in the sacraments, then what will become of us? Yea, I say, let us consider this vital point before the opportunity be taken away.

The day of the Lord cometh as a thief in the night. From this same unexpectedness of His second coming our Lord Himself draws for us Christians a saving warning: *Watch, therefore, for ye know not what hour your Lord doth come.* Do not be led away by curiosity or credulity, and beware of such ones who pretend to know more than Christ hath granted them to know. Let us endeavor rather to know what failings we have, to number our transgressions, and to seek a limit to them in repentance. Let us take heed lest the children of this world and our own passions lull our spirits into sleep, till the approach of that longed for, yet dreadful hour: *When the Lord come.*

The blessing of the Lord come upon you by His grace and love towards man, always, now, and ever and unto the ages of the ages.

Sermon Preached on Trinity Sunday

There are three that bear record in heaven, the Father, the Word, and the Holy Spirit; and these three are one (1 John 5:7).

The Orthodox Faith is this, that we worship One God in Trinity, and the Trinity in Unity, neither confounding the persons (hypostasis), nor dividing the substance (Symbol d'Athanasius). What will it profit us when we study deeply concerning the Trinity, if we be found lacking in humility and thereby are displeasing to the Most Holy Trinity? It is not for us to search into the incomprehensible mystery of Divinity. If we would approach anywhere within a reasonable approach to the Divine Mind, we, who *are of the lower ones*, should always endeavor to be pleasing companions to those *who are of the higher ones*, so that we may fervently glorify the thrice illumined Deity together with the angels, singing with that *faith, which is the assurance of things hoped for, the best of things not seen: Holy, Holy, Holy, Lord of Sabbath, heaven and earth are full of Thy glory.*

"Some may say," as St. Cyril of Jerusalem has long ago rightly surmised, "if the nature or substance of God is infinite, then to what purpose do we speak of it? But shall I abstain from taking water out of the river for my use, though a small measure, because I cannot drink up the whole river? Is it because my eyes cannot contain the whole of the sun himself, I should not, as much as is necessary, make use of the daylight? And if I were to enter some large garden, the fruits of which I could not eat up, would you, for this reason, have me leave the garden altogether hungry?" Indeed, we need the water, we need the sunlight, and the fruits of good endeavor and religious labor we enjoy. Therefore, we should, and it is our bounden duty to learn of that knowledge, which the Creator has been pleased to reveal of Himself to His Church, *without giving ourselves to vain speculations, and probing into mysteries* not necessary for our temporal welfare, much less so for our eternal salvation; and while not attainable to our limited mind, sometimes because of the presence of sinful pride, sometimes on account of deceit and feeble support in false systems and individual schemes, but chiefly because a drop does not contain the ocean, a particle of creation cannot embrace the earth, the worlds, and that wisdom and power which ordered the universe and established the laws by which it is preserved.

To learn of the Supreme Being and concerning the Holy Trinity in the Godhead, we need not go far; the philosopher cannot make clearer the light itself; we need not question the astronomer; and surely the majority of mankind only become puzzled when they singly weigh the corroborations of the geologist. Just look around and you will see on the space of a few yards of earth a great quantity of heterogeneous beings and natures, existing in the same air and by the same material food in substance as we do; yet some are adapted to life in the air, some move only in the water, and others are subjected to several certain limited forms of existence upon the land, while man, by his intellect and by his will, adapts himself to his surroundings in such a measure that he controls all other forms of animal life, and even overcomes natural obstacles by a force which is above nature. Thus we see man is created in the likeness of the Most High Creator.

After all these ages we cannot find in the advanced theories of modern literature an hypothesis that may compare with the plain statement of facts by the Holy Fathers during the first centuries of Christianity, as we have them concisely epitomized by St. John of Damascus. He says: "The Divinity is indescribable and incomprehensible. For *no one knoweth the Son, but the Father, and the Father no one knoweth save the Son* (Matt. 11:27). And also the Holy Spirit knoweth that which is of God, as the spirit of man knoweth the things of a man (1 Cor. 2:11). Beside the first and blessed Being, no one ever knew God, unless God had revealed Himself to someone; no one, not only of mankind, but no one of the celestial powers, nor of the Cherubim and Seraphim. Yet God has not left us entirely ignorant of Himself. The very knowledge of the existence of God the Creator has Himself implanted in our nature. And creation itself, the government of nature and its preservation proclaim the greatness of God. Above this, first through the law and the Prophets, then through His only begotten Son, our Lord and Savior Jesus Christ, God revealed to us as much knowledge of Himself as we are capable of containing. Therefore, all that has been given us by the law, the Prophets, the Apostles, and the Evangelists, we accept, acknowledge, and respect, and we seek nothing more. Thus God, as the Omniscient One and the Provider of that which is profitable for each one of us, has revealed all that is for our good, and kept in silence that which we are not capable of containing. Being satisfied thereby, we will keep to this, not transfixing the borders of eternity and not overstepping Divine tradition."

In the light of Divine Revelation, it becomes clear to our reason that, excepting the one, true, most perfect God, another cannot exist, because the most wise, most powerful, the most High and perfect Being must be only one, beside whom there is no other.

The Christian Faith is the religion of the Most Holy Trinity. And this is nowhere so plainly demonstrated as it is in the books of the New Testament. The preacher with the hearers and doers of the Word would be unequal to the task to take up at this moment for examination the great number of testimonies we have in the history of the New Testament concerning the Orthodox Faith, in which we worship One God in Trinity and the Trinity in Unity. But this is not all. If you turn to the books of the Old Testament, it can be seen that the Patriarchs of the nations and the saints of old had almost as clear a conception of the nature of God as we Christians, and believing in One God they at the same time worshipped, more or less consciously, the Father, the Son, and the Holy Spirit. The Most Holy Trinity, while distinct in Persons, is of equal Divine Substance, and equal Majesty. We do not belittle the awful magnitude of this Truth when we follow the example of the Holy Fathers by taking various illustrations from created life to help us in some measure grasp this doctrine of the Divine Three in One, and One in Three. In man's soul, the image of God is more or less reflected. Take, for instance, the memory which recalls the hour of Divine Liturgy, the understanding which reasons upon the duty of public prayer, or considers the excuses that might be pleaded for staying at home, and then the will which chooses one course or the other.

And now let us remember that, although we are among the weakest members of all creation, *we may become, by being faithful Christians, partakers of the Divine Nature* (2 Peter 1:4) *that by the grace of the Holy Spirit, who has regenerated us, we are all the children of the Heavenly Father and brethren to His only begotten Son* (John 1:12, 13; Luke 13:21). Thus we may come into the closest moral relations with the Triune God Himself, if only, believing in Him and earnestly drawing toward Him with hope, we shall love Him *with our whole heart, with our whole soul, and with our whole mind* (Matt. 22:27). Then, without doubt, the promise of the Savior will be fulfilled for us. *Jesus said: If a man love Me, he will keep My word, and My Father will love him, and will come unto him, and make Our abode with him* (John 14:13). And then also we will understand the meaning of these words of the Apostle: *Know ye not that ye are a temple of God, and that the Spirit of God dwelleth in you?* (1 Cor. 3:16). Amen.

The Condition of Society

How long will it thus go on! When will the baptized become active Christians, so that the pastors may give their attention to the conversion of the heathen? What a terrible battle we must fight. Already the fire of hell is in the world. Great cities are multiplying throughout the land. The farmer, as the word is defined in our dictionaries, is a thing of the past. It is now the land-owner with a mansion in the city, a yacht on the sea, and with a private train across the continent. There are comparatively but a few laborers in the fields — too poor to support families. The quiet country homes are becoming few, shall I say precious? I fear not so, because people are fast losing their ability to rightly estimate the value of things. Most of the cities in all the world are overcrowded. The female portion of the population is most conspicuous. A stupid craze after unwholesome fashions is the one all-absorbing passion of the majority of women. There is no room for gardens and yards; most of the children in San Francisco are actually brought up in the streets. Oh, how few of them feel the blessed influence of a Christian home! Young men and young women are continually "on the go," as they say. And this "go" is a nervous, unsteady rush to "keep up with the times." And after all their hurry nothing is left but steam and vapor, for they are empty, as empty as the changing and vanishing world can be. Yet they fret and inquire: "Where shall we go to and what shall we see? What shall we do? Oh! What can we do?" If you promenade along the broad avenue or pass through the narrow lane, if you visit the meeting halls in the city or look into the factories, everywhere you see that same all-devouring gaze of the bold young woman, who stares with a kind of artificial movement of the eyes. And sometimes you hear even so-called Christians say that it is a weakness of character in one who has the downcast eyes of modesty, the blush of innocence. Such people do not know the live sense and fine impulse of a pure conscience. When a young man puffs tobacco smoke or shows his teeth with a disapproving smile in the presence of and at the conversation of older people, then society is wrong; something is the matter with his family.

In view of all this, beloved, the preacher of the Word of God is obliged by a terrible oath he has given before he received the gift in Apostolic succession at his ordination, to present to you the whole of the Truth, not a part of it.

The number of unmarried people is increasing. And there are some married people who say: "We do not want children, because we want to have as much pleasure as possible." This is a false position, for in a Christian marriage one kind of pleasure is not allowed continually. Christians marry for the sake of God and His law as much as they do for themselves. But Christians who remain single renounce marriage and live holy for the sake of God and Him alone. Thus we find that the family tie is abused, as well as the single state. Courtship of young people just out of school is not to be advised, because it often leads to debauchery. A courtship running through long years also gives occasion to sin and a species of wrongdoing to God, for the heart and its love are stolen from God and thrown away on a man.

Throughout all the long centuries of Christianity there have been in the Church heroic members, young people of both sexes, who by the grace of God have kept their souls pure and intact, and have dedicated to the honor of God the noblest attribute of their human life, namely, an untarnished purity of soul and body. Such persons have had the courage and such unbounded confidence in God's assistance that, although living in the world and its dangers, though threatened by the cravings of their own individual passions and by the temptations of the devil, yet they have succeeded bravely in preserving this treasure even in a frail earthen vessel, have carried it uninjured through life's long journey here below, and have finally presented it to their Lord.

Christian heroes and heroines, you who have imitated or who still do imitate the sublime example of the Most Blessed Virgin, the Church admires your spirit of sacrifice as she does that of the holy martyrs, who in a few hours finished their contest and proved their fidelity to God and their faith; because you have to combat, to suffer, and to sacrifice your whole life through. With joy and veneration do the angels look down upon you, for you resemble themselves. With motherly affection and with mighty power does the Holy Virgin Mary when you earnestly pray throw her sheltering omophorion around you, for you are her pupils and imitators. With the sweetness of divine love the heavenly Bridegroom will fill your heart and more than compensate you for the fleeting, transient, worldly love that you have laid down at His feet. The eternal Judge will find you waiting like the wise and prudent virgins who all through life carry in their hands the pure oblation of love and the burning light of good example. Therefore, faithful to the end, He will invite you to the eternal wedding feast in heaven. Amen.

Sermon to Those Preparing for Holy Communion

Let a man examine himself, and so let him eat of that bread, and drink of that cup. For he that eateth and drinketh unworthily, eateth and drinketh damnation unto himself.

(1 Cor. 11:28, 29)

These words of the Apostle are terrible, and so are they as the truth unfailing. Verily the judgment is heavy and the damnation terrible for the one who receives the body and blood of Christ without due honor and without such a disposition of the spirit as is required. A terrible judgment has befell that apostate people who sentenced our Lord Jesus Christ to be crucified, when they cried: *His blood be on us and on our children* (Matt.). But that unfortunate people did not know the mystery of the incarnation of the Son of God, and committed that greatest crime in blindness and ignorance: *For had they known,* says St. Paul, *they should not have crucified the Lord of Glory. Of how much sorer punishment, suppose ye, shall be worthy of such an one,* who was born in Christianity, from childhood taught in the mysteries of the faith, and notwithstanding all this, hath — by light-heartedness and carelessness — *trodden underfoot the Son of God, and hath counted the blood of the covenant, wherewith he was sanctified, an unholy thing, and hath done despite unto the spirit of grace* (Heb. 10:29).

Hence the reason why the Church with such care strives to prepare us for the reception of the life-giving mysteries of Christ by fast, prayer, repentance. After a few moments when the cup of the covenant shall be brought out, unto which we must approach in order to reanimate within us, renew and strengthen our covenant with Jesus Christ, we will hear the last call of the Church which summons thus:

With fear of God and faith approach ye. In those sacred moments let be hushed within us all other thoughts, let be banished from our souls all other feelings, besides those unto which the Holy Church would elevate our spirits. *Let us draw near with fear of God, faith and love, that we may be partakers of the life eternal.*

That we may inspire within us that sacred fear, let us consider: Where are we now? Before whom do we stand? Unto what do we approach? Where are we? *Moses, Moses,* called God to His selected leader of Israel, *draw not nigh hither: put off thy shoes from off thy feet, for the place whereon thou standest is holy ground* (Ex. 3:5). Since the place unto which God once descended has become sanctified, and to which the man who was called the friend of God could not approach without care, then how much holier is the place which is sanctified by such often repeated descensions of the Holy Spirit at the consecration of the terrible mysteries upon which even the angels look with fear.

Before whom do we stand? It is the God of unapproachable glory, from whose presence it was once that Mt. Sinai blazed and trembled; the God Almighty, who spake and it was done; He commanded, and it stood fast; that which is not, He nameth a thing existing; He maketh to die and maketh to live; He lowereth unto hell and raiseth up again; the God All-holy, who bears not with iniquity and shuns unrighteousness; the Lord, a jealous God, who exacts of children the sins of fathers even unto the third and fourth generations; the God All-righteous, who came down to see the wickedness of the citizens of Sodom and Gomorrah, and which cities the heavenly flame swallowed up. It is true that God appears to us here in His body and blood, without external grandeur and glory, without terrible manifestations; for, were it otherwise, we would say as the Israelites had said: *Let not God speak with us, lest we die* (Exod.).

Unto what do we approach? To the Divine Body, which Simeon, the saintly old man, had once received in his hands with holy fear; to the Divine Body, by the touch of which the sick were healed, the leprous cleansed, and which the demons feared; before the nakedness and wounds of which the sun darkened, the earth quaked, the

rocks brake; to the most Glorious Body, which ascended into the
heavens and upon which the Cherubim and the Seraphim look with
fear. True it is that it appears to us in the form of common food, but
were it otherwise we would say with Peter: *Depart from me, for I am
a sinful man, O Lord!* (Matt. 5:8). And so it is here we stand, such
is the presence we stand before, and such is that unto which we approach. Great is the gift we receive from the hand of the Lord. Holy
is His most pure body, holy is His life-creating blood, and therefore,
let us approach the cup of the covenant with greater care and more
fear that we may not be scorched with its flame, that we may receive
the flesh and blood of Christ not unto judgment and condemnation,
but unto the cleansing, the sanctification, and the enlivening of our
nature decaying in sin. Amen.

Address on Christmas Day

The Orthodox Catholic Church celebrates today the nativity of our Lord and Savior Jesus Christ.

Christmas day is generally observed as a holiday throughout the world. And verily it should be a day of rejoicing. I say rejoice, for, glory to God in the highest, we are now enabled to obtain peace on earth, as the good will of our Creator and Judge has been proclaimed to all men.

Unfortunately, we now often see in the world a decline in religious celebrations of Christian festivals,[7] just as in political and civil holidays we now often notice a tendency to withdraw from public scenes to one's own narrow sphere of privacy, personal comfort, and individual satisfaction. Such conditions are detrimental to society at large. The first cause of it all is the family — the home from which all men and women take into the world the form of their future character. The nation which is devoid of lessons in religion and patriotism in the family — which is the fountain source of all learning — such a nation is going to destruction.

Since we today magnify Christ, the giver of life, who now was born in the flesh for our sake of the unwedded and most pure Virgin Mary, we may most appropriately, as duty bound, consider the worth of our celebration. When we hear the teaching of Him who today was a little child seeking shelter with the cattle and sheep, and remember

---

[7] The majority of churches in San Francisco (as is the general rule in America) are closed and have no purely religious services whatever on the 25th of December.

that He said, *I am the way, and the life, and the truth*, and also, *the truth will make you free*, we are impressed with the exalted character of Him whose mission it was and is to gather all mankind into the one fold of the Only Shepherd. And our Lord says the truth will save us. We must study the truth to the full measure of our competency, and know our Lord Jesus Christ the Savior. We must use our God-given intellect and discern true doctrine from falsehood. We must worship God with our whole being, body and soul, consequently we develop our reason (as our faith grows stronger) and praise the Lord understandingly. For when we worship with the inspiring feeling of our heart only, we bring a half offering. The offering must be whole.

When we study the different forms of worship of different people who are considered Christians, we see that some bow in adoration with fervent devotion, while others with exultant heart sing loud praise, as if carried away in ecstasy, depriving the spirit of one of its faculties, i.e., adoration. Now, this is according to science, and those who have studied psychology know it. True and complete science is always compatible with religion. The Orthodox and Apostolic Church has ever held that man must offer praise from a warm heart while devoutly adoring the Sublime both physically and spiritually, and at the same time following truthful doctrine. Yes, we must seek and study the truth. I do not say we can at once perfectly know it, for we must first comprehend God, who is the truth. When we become Christ-like we know the truth, and the truth makes us free.

The Church is the treasure house of God upon earth. I offer these precious gems to you, hoping you will take them away to your homes, safely guarded in a grateful heart, and earnestly ponder over them, seeking God in prayer accompanied by a pure life. For only then we may enter into the true spirit of this celebration and rightly comprehend the hymn we sing: "Christ is born! Ye faithful, glorify! Christ from the heavens, Oh come to greet Him! Christ upon the earth, be ye lifted on high! Sing to the Lord, all the earth! And in gladness praise Him. O ye nations! for He hath been glorified!" Amen.

CPSIA information can be obtained at www.ICGtesting.com
Printed in the USA
BVOW051600301011

274851BV00001B/32/P